NEW YORK CITY

New York City: The Basics offers an accessible look at the dynamic and diverse hub of New York City. Written in a clear, engaging style, the book discusses geographic, historic, demographic, socioeconomic, housing, and governmental aspects of the Big Apple.

Since the mid-20th century, New York City has been competing against other global and major cities, including London and Tokyo, primarily driven by global financial and securities markets. Its enormous concentration of capital, as well as its varied and resilient economy, has contributed to its prominent status and its glittering skyline, exemplifying the city's transition from blue-collar manufacturing to a knowledge-based economy. As a cultural capital, the city encompasses an extensive cluster of publishing companies, high-end shopping, a wide variety of unique art scenes, and a pulsating nightlife that includes Broadway shows, exhibits, and fashion events. The chapters touch on different topics, from the history to the demography and immigration, the economy, housing, government and governance, and the city's exceptionalism, ending with an overview of the five boroughs of the city.

This book serves as a valuable guide for undergraduate and graduate students in geography, urban studies, urban affairs, and urban planning, and would be an excellent resource for anyone planning a field trip to New York City.

Katrin B. Anacker is currently a professor at the Schar School of Policy and Government at George Mason University, VA, USA.

THE BASICS SERIES

The Basics is a highly successful series of accessible guidebooks which provide an overview of the fundamental principles of a subject area in a jargon-free and undaunting format.

Intended for students approaching a subject for the first time, the books both introduce the essentials of a subject and provide an ideal springboard for further study. With over 50 titles spanning subjects from artificial intelligence (AI) to women's studies, *The Basics* are an ideal starting point for students seeking to understand a subject area.

Each text comes with recommendations for further study and gradually introduces the complexities and nuances within a subject.

LIBERTARIANISM
Jessica Flanigan and Christopher Freiman

CLOSE READING (SECOND EDITION)
David Greenham

FEMINISM
Renee Heberle

MINDFULNESS
Sophie Sansom, David Shannon, and Taravajra

URBAN DESIGN
Tim Heath and Florian Wiedmann

PUBLIC RELATIONS (SECOND EDITION)
Deborah Silverman

EDUCATION STUDIES
Catherine Simon

DRAG
Mark Edward and Chris Greenough#

BIOANTHROPOLOGY
Marc Kissel

NEW YORK CITY
KATRIN B. ANACKER

For more information about this series, please visit: www.routledge.com/The-Basics/book-series/B

"NYC's story is the story of U.S. cities generally, from its history and dynamic early growth, to its economic transformation and the ascendance of neoliberal urbanism and austerity politics, to the spread of gentrification, and the housing woes of contemporary times. Katrin Anacker's book provides the foundation for comprehending New York in all of its dimensions and as such is an indispensable tool for anyone, student or scholar, seeking to understand this most important of U.S. cities."

–Edward Goetz, Professor, University of Minnesota, author of *The One-Way Street of Integration: Fair Housing and the Pursuit of Racial Justice in American Cities*

"Katrin Anacker breaks down the colossus of Gotham into digestible bites. Lifetime New Yorkers, recent migrants, and urban experts alike will find something to chew on in this accessible book that covers the city's history, geography, economics and its pivotal, unique role in the nation and world. Anacker never loses sight of the big picture even when including an admirable level of detail – locals and visitors alike will learn that the city's festering garbage piles go back to plans laid in 1811! The book is very well-sourced and each chapter concludes with a short list of cities to learn more about the central topic, providing the reader with a nearly infinite set of rabbit holes to dive into."

–Michael Lens, Professor, UCLA, author of *Where the Hood At: Fifty Years of Change in Black Neighborhoods*

"There are many books written about New York City's neighborhoods, history, economy, politics, housing, transportation, and geography. What makes *New York City: The Basics* unique is that it incorporates essential knowledge about all these social domains into one intricately detailed, well-structured and clearly written scholarly work. It is astonishing to me how many distinct sources of information Katrin Anacker has surveyed, investigated, scrutinized, selected from, and expertly organized. The book offers a complex mosaic of all significant aspects of urban life and can serve as an encyclopedic source of reference to one of the most mesmerizing, conflicted, divided, yet energizing and beloved metropolises in the world."

–**Elena Vesselinov,** Associate Professor,
City University of New York

"Katrin B. Anacker's *New York City: The Basics* is a succinct and readable primer on the evolution of the city, starting from its early history to now. It draws from multiple academic disciplines to highlight the importance of geographic location for its development as a global economic center, explains the role of immigration in creating its rich demographic diversity, and provides background on the city's struggles with housing supply."

–**Rachael Woldoff,** Professor, West Virginia University,
author of *Priced Out: Stuyvesant Town and the Loss of
Middle-Class Neighborhoods*

"Anacker has created a demographic, economic, and cultural survey of New York City that seamlessly links the remarkable evolution of this phenomenal place with its present character. Wonderfully concise and immensely satisfying."

–**Laura Wolf-Powers,** Professor,
City University of New York, author of
*University City: History, Race and Community in
the Era of the Innovation District*

NEW YORK CITY

THE BASICS

Katrin B. Anacker

NEW YORK AND LONDON

Designed cover image: Getty Images

First published 2026
by Routledge
605 Third Avenue, New York, NY 10158

and by Routledge
4 Park Square, Milton Park, Abingdon, Oxon, OX14 4RN

Routledge is an imprint of the Taylor & Francis Group, an informa business

© 2026 Katrin B. Anacker

The right of Katrin B. Anacker to be identified as author of this work has been asserted in accordance with sections 77 and 78 of the Copyright, Designs and Patents Act 1988.

All rights reserved. No part of this book may be reprinted or reproduced or utilized in any form or by any electronic, mechanical, or other means, now known or hereafter invented, including photocopying and recording, or in any information storage or retrieval system, without permission in writing from the publishers.

For Product Safety Concerns and Information please contact our EU representative GPSR@taylorandfrancis.com. Taylor & Francis Verlag GmbH, Kaufingerstraße 24, 80331 München, Germany.

Trademark notice: Product or corporate names may be trademarks or registered trademarks, and are used only for identification and explanation without intent to infringe.

ISBN: 978-1-041-03527-5 (hbk)
ISBN: 978-1-041-03519-0 (pbk)
ISBN: 978-1-003-62417-2 (ebk)

DOI: 10.1201/9781003624172

Typeset in Bembo
by Newgen Publishing UK

CONTENTS

	Overview of Chapters	ix
	Acknowledgments	xi
1	Introduction	1
2	Location	5
3	History	10
4	Demography and Immigration	25
5	Economy	33
6	Housing	47
7	Government and Governance	62
8	New York City's Exceptionalism	69
9	New York City's Five Boroughs: Brooklyn, Manhattan, the Bronx, Queens, and Staten Island	86

10 Conclusion **99**

References 102
Index 124

OVERVIEW OF CHAPTERS

New York City: The Basics discusses geographic, historic, demographic, socioeconomic, and housing aspects in New York City, along with its exceptionalism. Chapter 1 briefly introduces the United States' capital of capitalism and its role as media destination, cultural capital, and fashion center, all creating the home of a dynamic, diverse, and amazingly rich collection of people and neighborhoods, characterized by never-ending change.

Chapter 2 elaborates on New York City's location on the Atlantic seaboard, the Hudson River, and the East River, which have shaped its local and regional economic development.

Chapter 3 presents New York City's history that includes the Leni Lenape, New York's native tribe, the Dutch West India Company (WIC), Peter Stuyvesant's tenure as director general of New Amsterdam, Governor John Montgomerie's adoption of a new municipal charter, and the Plan of 1811, which has provided the city's foundation for urban growth and continues to shape land use and development to the present day.

Chapter 4 discusses New York City's population development and its resiliency over time, facilitated by the incorporation of the five boroughs in 1898. It also discusses its racial and ethnic diversity as well as its role as the quintessential U.S. immigrant city.

Chapter 5 elaborates on New York City's premier global status among major cities. It also discusses its municipal fiscal crisis of the mid- to late 1970s which was the largest citywide fiscal crisis in U.S. history.

Chapter 6 discusses the many factors that have influenced New York City's housing supply and housing demand, its imbalance between the two, and the outcomes of these factors for homeowners and renters.

Chapter 7 is about government and governance in New York City, focusing on the role of the mayor and the New York City Council. It also discusses the Port Authority of New York and New Jersey (PANYNJ) and its massive infrastructure portfolio.

Chapter 8 focuses on New York City's exceptionalism, partly due to its long history of liberalism and leftism, its decades-long, vigorous local civic boosterism, and its so-called "growth machine" (Molotch, 1976), driven by the political, business, media, and cultural establishments, as well as its many real estate families, local economic development, and marketing and tourism organizations.

Chapter 9 discusses New York City's five boroughs.

Chapter 10 concludes, with a discussion of New York City's past, current, and future paths in terms of demography, economics, and housing, and its two major challenges: climate change and socioeconomic inequality.

ACKNOWLEDGMENTS

Over the past few years, many colleagues have supported this project. Alan Mallach went above and beyond, providing many constructive and welcome comments on a previous draft. Daniel Campo treated my writing as his own and provided many superb suggestions on a previous draft as well. Thank you! Despite all of my colleagues' constructive comments, all errors and mistakes remain mine.

Several individuals were directly and indirectly involved with this manuscript. At Routledge, Ed Needle and then Emily Irvine provided much appreciated guidance. My invaluable personal copy editor Matt Ogborn improved several earlier drafts. Helen McManus, Kimberly MacVaugh, Chris Magee, and Lorena Jordan, all Policy and Government Librarians on George Mason University's Arlington campus, answered my many requests for assistance and found me some hidden gems. Rajendra Kulkarni helpfully created the two figures in Chapter 2. Sarah Johnson, a former dissertation and thesis specialist affiliated with George Mason University's Writing Center, was kind enough to check my references section in an earlier draft three times.

Several individuals were also indirectly involved with my manuscript. On George Mason University's Arlington campus, colleague Robert Deitz kept me well-fed and in good spirits, and Jim Finkelstein and Jim Pfiffner provided much-appreciated mentoring. All three have a great sense of humor that kept me going. Kingsley Haynes and Jim Finkelstein hired me during the Great Recession, when I needed a new academic home at very short notice. I cannot imagine where I would now be without that sponsor letter, work visa, and letter of offer!

Colleagues Alan Abramson, Desmond Dinan, Anne Holton, Jim Olds, and Judith Wilde occasionally checked in on me, making sure I was well. Arlington County's Department of Parks and Recreation provides an award-winning, wonderful, interconnected trail system, including the lovely Bluemont Junction Trail, the delightful Four Mile Run Trail, and the efficient W&OD Trail ("passing on your left!"), enabling me to hash things out during rejuvenating late-afternoon runs. Thank you! Lastly, I dedicate this book to my parents, Jürgen and Erika Anacker, who have been supporting me in innumerable ways over many, many years. Thanks to their very hard work and great support, I am where I am today. *Und wie immer—nein, ihr braucht auch dieses Buch nicht zu lesen.*

INTRODUCTION

New York City has been praised by many writers and thinkers for more than a century. Mayor Fiorello LaGuardia exclaimed in the mid-1940s that "there is only one New York City in the whole world and there is nothing like it" (Hanlon, 2017, p. 2). In her essay "My Home Town" published in *McCall's* magazine, intellectual Dorothy Parker (1928, n.p.) offered the following reflection:

> London is satisfied, Paris is resigned, but New York is always hopeful. Always it believes that something good is about to come off, and it must hurry to meet it. There is excitement ever running its streets. Each day, as you go out, you feel the little nervous quiver that is yours when you sit in the theater just before the curtain rises. Other places may give you a sweet and soothing sense of level; but in New York there is always the feeling of "Something's going to happen." It isn't peace. But, you know, you do get used to peace, and so quickly. And you never get used to New York.

In his 1949 book *Here is New York*, writer E. B. White called New York the "loftiest of cities" (quoted in Mollenkopf, 1992, p. 10), further suggesting that "New York is to the nation what the white church is to the village—the visible symbol of aspiration and faith, the white plume saying the way is up" (quoted in Sagalyn, 2016, p. xv). O. Henry, liberally paraphrased by *The New York Times*, stated that "While all cities say the same thing, New York says it first" (quoted by Revell, 2003, frontispiece). Similarly,

Thomas Kessner (2003, p. xvi) exclaimed that bustling "Gotham was the central nervous system for the entire system of cities in the United States." William Helmreich summed up New York City, "the world's greatest outdoor museum" (2023, p. xxix), as follows:

> New York is a city with a dynamic, diverse, and amazingly rich collection of people and neighborhoods whose members display both small-town values and a high degree of sophistication. This stems from living in a very modern, technologically advanced, and world-class city that is the epitome of the twenty-first century.
>
> (2013, p. 2)

In 2010, UN Under-Secretary-General Brian Urquhart stated that "New York is a grand, hard, gritty place where no one underestimates their own importance or overestimates anyone else's" (Hanlon, 2017, p. 2). Finally, Mike Wallace (2017, p. 7), reflecting on New York City in the 1920s, mentions

> the basket of blue ribbons accumulated at the national level. New York [...] had the country's biggest port, bank, insurance company, and dry-goods wholesaler, [...] it was the nation's urban consumer market. It boasted the USA's largest corporation, museum, theater, racetrack, baseball stadium, sugar refinery, building contractor, railroad bridge, Catholic orphanage, high school, university, restaurant, subway system, police force, prison population, system of charities, public workforce, and municipal debt.

Others have called New York City "Metropolis of the Western World" and the "City of Dreadful Height" (Blake, 2020, p. 1).

Interestingly, in the late 18th and 19th centuries, Philadelphia and New York City competed against each other, but many observers realized that New York City was better positioned for generating a national or even international reputation (Hood, 2017; Wallace, 2017). Due to its location, its historical experiences, its unique attributes, and its infrastructure, including its port, New York City was "[w]eeks ahead of rivals in other ports," as "Manhattan's businessmen learned the latest intelligence on overseas cotton prices or the vote on English tariff" (Kessner,

2003, p. 7). Indeed, "no other city in the country was receiving better information about distant markets and conditions, or getting it faster—or making more money from it" (Burrows & Wallace, 1999, pp. 439–440).

In 1898, artist John Sloan, who grew up in Philadelphia but later moved to New York, stated that "'a good thing done in Philadelphia is well-done in Philadelphia' but [that] 'a good thing done in New York is heralded abroad'" (Wallace, 2017, p. 866). In sum, in the late 19th and early 20th centuries, New York City became the de facto capital of the United States (Blake, 2020).

Currently, some see New York as "a cultural Mecca founded on transgression and innovation," as evidenced by the city's remarkable range, from high-end shopping, Broadway shows, and its glittering skyline to gritty, diverse low-income neighborhoods (Greenberg, 2008, p. 8). For others, New York City is the nation's capital of capitalism, its media destination, its cultural capital, and its fashion center (Hum, 2014; Jennings, 2018; Plotch, 2020). In sum, New York City may be seen as the nation's economic powerhouse or engine and the nation's financial hub, as exemplified by the comparison that it has 2.6% of the nation's population yet generates 4.3% of the national gross national product (GNP), as stated by Mayor Michael Bloomberg in November 2012, right after Superstorm Sandy (Berg, 2018).

New York City has attracted passionate and talented, creative people eager to advance their careers and be a part of the collective urban endeavor. Its ambition is its characteristic spirit, which may have contributed to New York City's extreme forms of individualism but also civicism, or civic-mindedness (i.e., a strong, underlying sense of community and neighborhood attachment; Bell & de-Shalit, 2011).

New York City has also been characterized by never-ending change (Hamill, 2004). As stated in an 1856 issue of *Harper's Monthly*, "New York is notoriously the largest and least loved of any of our great cities. Why should it be loved as a city? It is never the same city for a dozen years together" (Burrows & Wallace, 1999, p. 695; Hood, 2017). In 2002, after the September 11, 2001 attacks, architect and writer James Sanders stated "No city on earth could match the energy New York displayed in remaking itself to meet the challenges of modern life—nor the brilliance, daring and, in most cases, speed with which it carried out that remaking" (Sanders, 2002, n.p.).

Over time, New York City has had many nicknames, including "Gotham" ("Goats' Town" in old Anglo-Saxon), first used by Washington Irving in his satirical periodical *Salmagundi* (1807) and then by the radical ethnic press. Another nickname is the "Big Apple," which originated in horse racing in the 1920s but was supposedly adopted by the jazz community to capture "playing in the big time" (Steinberg, 2014, p. 284) and also gained popularity in the 1970s. "Naked City" was inspired by film noir, and "Fun City" was coined by Mayor John Lindsay during a live television interview at the time of the 12-day-long transit strike in 1966. Other nicknames are "New Rome," inspired by the city's many modern art openings and high fashion designers; "the ungovernable city"; "the rotten apple"; the dystopian "asphalt jungle"; and "Capital of the World," popularized by E. B. White in the mid-20th century and by Mayor Rudolph Giuliani in the 1990s (Hanlon, 2017; Helmreich, 2013).

FURTHER INFORMATION

Dyja, T. (2021). *New York, New York, New York: Four decades of success, excess, and transformation*. Simon & Schuster.

Helmreich, W. B. (2013). *The New York nobody knows: Walking 6,000 miles in the city*. Princeton University Press.

Steinberg, T. (2014). *Gotham unbound: The ecological history of greater New York*. Simon & Schuster.

LOCATION

New York City is part of the New York–Newark–Jersey City, New York–New Jersey–Pennsylvania Metropolitan Statistical Area (MSA), which encompasses four metropolitan divisions (Lakewood–New Brunswick, New Jersey; Nassau County–Suffolk County, New York; Newark, New Jersey; and New York–Jersey City–White Plains, New York–New Jersey) with 22 counties total, as shown in Figure 2.1 (U.S. Bureau of the Census, n.d.c). New York City consists of five boroughs: Brooklyn, Manhattan, the Bronx, Queens, and Staten Island, as shown in Figure 2.2.

This book only focuses on New York City, as its exceptionalism (discussed in detail in Chapter 8) primarily applies to the city, not the MSA or the wider region, including Connecticut and the Hudson Valley.

New York City's raison d'etre is its Atlantic seaboard location, along a 585-mile-long, deep, and calm waterfront with many rivers, islands, and bays and only about 20 miles from the Atlantic Ocean through the Long Island Sound, which enabled the development of port facilities beneficial for trade and offered shorter routes to Philadelphia and other cities in the south, such as Savannah or New Orleans, as well as the lucrative West Indian markets, compared to Boston to the north (Flood, 2010; Melosi, 2020; Osman, 2011; Schlichting, 2019). They are protected from most North Atlantic storms, as they are north of the narrow opening between Brooklyn and Staten Island, compared to Philadelphia's port facilities, which are located about 100 miles from the Atlantic Ocean

DOI: 10.1201/9781003624172-2

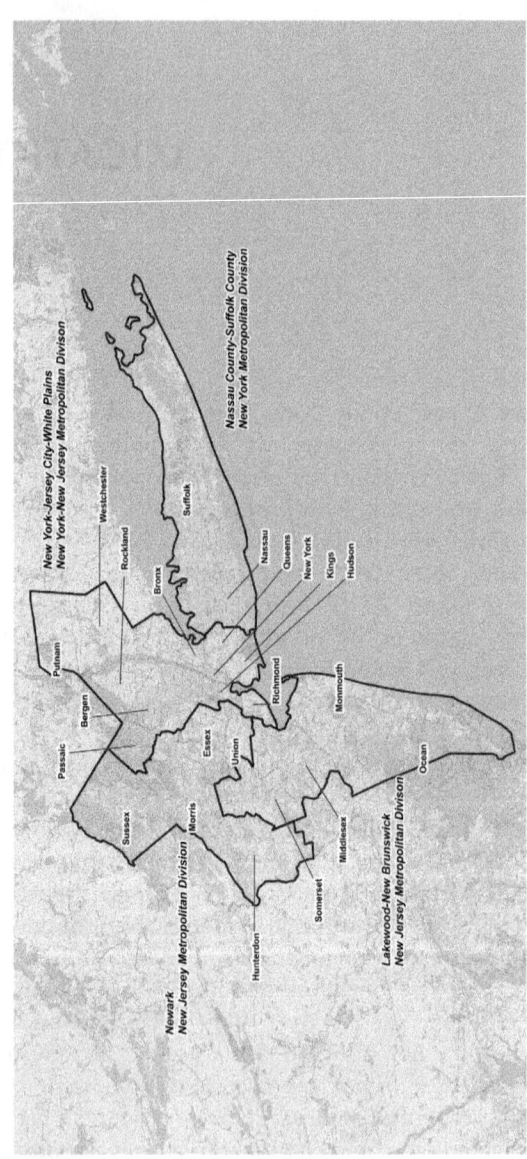

Figure 2.1 Overview of the New York–Newark–Jersey City, New York–New Jersey–Pennsylvania Metropolitan Statistical Area (MSA)

Source: author, based on U.S. Bureau of the Census, n.d.c. Map credit: Rajendra Kulkarni.

LOCATION 7

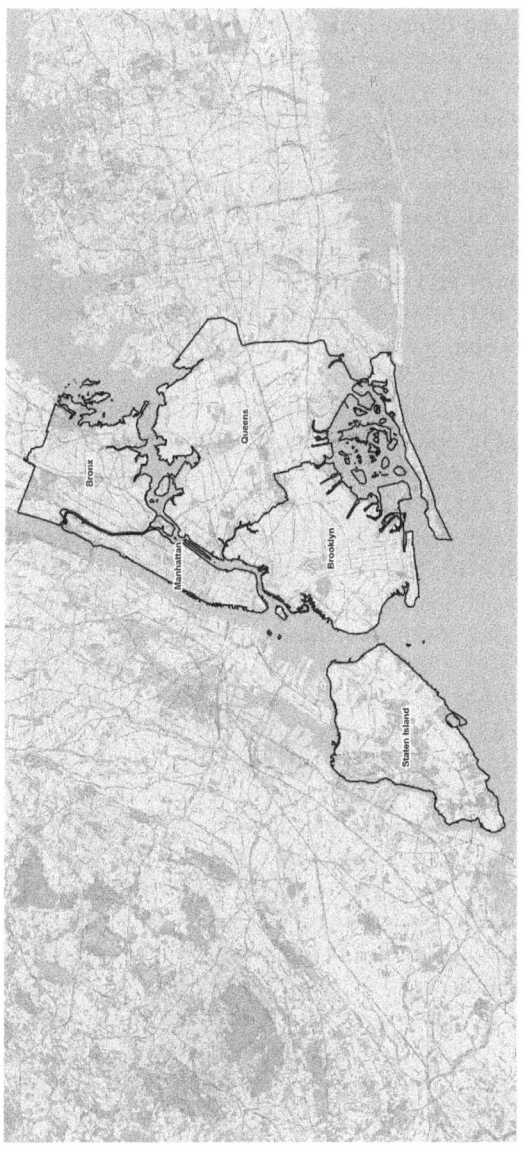

Figure 2.2 Overview of New York City's boroughs

Source: author, based on U.S. Bureau of the Census, n.d.c. Map credit: Rajendra Kulkarni.

(Jackson, 2007a). New York City's port facilities are not only much larger, deeper, and calmer but also less prone to ice compared to both Boston's and Philadelphia's harbors (Flood, 2010).

New York has benefitted from its location on the Hudson River estuary, where freshwater meets the Atlantic Ocean on a river that is more than 300 miles long and navigable, as well as the ice-free East River (Johnson, 1996). The tidal estuary has surging currents, enabling the greatest concentration of shipbuilding facilities on the East Coast for more than a century (Melosi, 2020; Steinberg, 2014). In 1818, New York City established regularly scheduled shipping services to Liverpool ("packet ships"; Bell & de-Shalit, 2011; Hood, 2017). New York has also benefitted from the Erie Canal Commission, established by New York State in 1810, which exploited the Hudson River and the broad plain between the river at Albany and Lake Erie before finding, building, and operating the Erie Canal in 1825 to connect the Hudson River to the Great Lakes and an inland, 363-mile canal system, allowing goods produced on the East Coast to be shipped further inland to the Midwest and West and shipped from the Midwestern grain belt to the East Coast through many other rivers and canals (Adams, 2014; Ballon, 2011c; Bender, 2002; Blake, 2020; Kessner, 2003). These developments not only decreased the costs of shipping goods but also helped New York City's financial market outperform its competitor Philadelphia by 1830 (Adams, 2014; Burrows & Wallace, 1999). New York City has also benefitted from the Croton Aqueduct, which has been distributing potable water from the Croton River in Westchester County to reservoirs in Manhattan since 1842, carrying water by gravity over about 40 miles and fostering population growth and urbanization (Macaulay-Lewis, 2021; Spady, 2020).

Around 1860, New York City's port facilities exported between one-third (Glaeser, 2005) and almost two-thirds (Macaulay-Lewis, 2021) of the nation's goods and imported about two-thirds of them, making it a boomtown (Glaeser, 2005). Around that time, the vast majority of federal government revenues came from customs duties from imported goods, about 80% of which were generated in New York City (Macaulay-Lewis, 2021). In 1897, about 4,000 ships unloaded their cargo per year (Burrows & Wallace, 1999). In 1900, New York City's port was the busiest port in the entire world (Caro, 1974), with enormous vessels making trans-Atlantic crossings and smaller ships plying domestic routes (Glaeser, 2005). The great activity at the port necessitated a complex economic ecosystem inhabited by diverse parties and facilitating job formation and economic growth. Upper-income merchants benefitted from the efforts of middle-income smiths or shipbuilders and lower-income laborers, stevedores, or dock workers, all clustered around the port (Barr, 2016). As an island city, New York City has taken much advantage of its waterfronts, port and shipbuilding facilities, and canal systems over the past few decades, but being an island has also posed disadvantages, requiring that ferries be taken or bridges and tunnels be constructed, facilitated by the Port Authority of New York and New Jersey (PANYNJ), discussed in Chapter 7 (Melosi, 2020).

FURTHER INFORMATION

Barr, J. M. (2016). *Building the skyline: The birth and growth of Manhattan's skyscrapers*. Oxford University Press.

Glaeser, E. L. (2005, December). *Urban colossus: Why is New York America's largest city?* https://www.newyorkfed.org/medialibrary/media/research/epr/05v11n2/0512glae.pdf

Gross, J. S., & Savitch, H. V. (2023). *New York*. Agenda Publishing.

Sorkin, M. (2009). *Twenty minutes in Manhattan*. North Point Press.

HISTORY

Starting about 12,000 years ago, the Leni Lenape, part of New York's large native Algonquin tribe, also known as the Delaware, fished in the salt marshes and hunted, and farmed wheat, maize, beans, and squash through an advanced slash-and-burn system while living in longhouses constructed of bent saplings covered with sheets of bark, the crevices plugged with clay and cornstalks; they provided shelter for up to a dozen of families located in Lenapehoking (Homeland of the Lenape) along the Atlantic seaboard from Long Island to Delaware (Azzarone, 2022; Legiardi-Laura, 2007; Manbeck, 2004; Melosi, 2020; Spady, 2020). Most natives moved from one place to the next every few months to take advantage of available firewood and arable land (Burrows & Wallace, 1999). When European explorers and then settlers arrived in the 1500s and 1600s, respectively, about 16,000 Leni Lenape resided in Lenapehoking in various tribes, groups, subgroups, and bands, with around 6,000 in 13 bands on Long Island alone, including the Montauk, the Shinnecock, the Unquachaug, the Secatogue, the Massapequa, the Merrick, the Rockaway, the Canarsee, the Matinecock, the Nissequogue, the Setaukets, the Corchaug, and the Manhanset, as well as the Weckquaesgecks from Westchester and some Mahicans from west of the river (Shepard & Noonan, 2018). Many of these band names are reflected in names of cities, villages, townships, and neighborhoods on Long Island and in the New York boroughs today (Heathcott, 2023; Helmreich, 2018).

In 1621, the Dutch West India Company (WIC), at the time one of the most powerful global trading monopolies for wine, beer, and distilled liquor, among other goods, established the colony New Netherland (Shorto, 2025; Steinberg, 2014). WIC was a company "in unbounded pursuit of money," not a religious sect or royal house (Flood, 2010, p. 133). It held a monopoly over all Dutch trade with West Africa and the Americas, making money through trade and by waging war on Spain (Burrows & Wallace, 1999; Shorto, 2025). In 1624, WIC proclaimed Provisional Orders that consisted of regulations and conditions for settlers, including establishing freedom and interest-free loans to purchase land, farm tools, and livestock on the one hand, and setting prices for acquired beaver pelts on the other (Angotti, 2008). Consistent with the Western concept of land ownership, the Dutch assumed that the land belonged to Native Americans. Thus, in 1626, Peter Minuit "purchased" New Amsterdam, now Manhattan, derived from the Algonquin name Mannahatta for "island of hills" (Sorkin, 2009, p. 95) or "island of many hills" (Sawadogo, 2022, p. 16) from one of the bands, the Canarsee Indians, for European knives, iron pots, beads, buttons, and other goods and trinkets, valued at 60 guilders, or the paltry sum of $24 (Shorto, 2025; Sorkin, 2009; Spady, 2020). From 1651 until 1664, Peter Stuyvesant served as director general of New Amsterdam, before establishing New Amsterdam's first municipal government in 1653 (Burrows & Wallace, 1999; Shorto, 2025). He appointed land surveyors to establish reliable property lines, laid out streets parallel to the waterfront, named streets, introduced cobblestones, banned garbage from the streets and established garbage disposal sites, designated fire wardens, established hanging fire buckets on street corners, and forbade the construction of wooden chimneys, thatched roofs, and haystacks (Burrows & Wallace, 1999; Johnson, 1996).

The Dutch ceded the land to the British in 1664, who renamed the settlement in honor of the Duke of York and lifted regulated food prices, creating a free market (Shorto, 2025). The new settlers had taken advantage of slavery since 1626, when multiple waves of African and Caribbean slaves arrived in New Netherland, where they were forced to work in agriculture and domestic households (Shepard & Noonan, 2018; Shorto, 2025). In the 1720s and 1730s, trade with the West Indies gradually increased, resulting in more slaves in Manhattan, first traded at the slave market at Wall Street and then working as stevedores, shipbuilders, coopers, carpenters, and butchers, among other professions (Burrows & Wallace, 1999; Hood, 2017; Shorto, 2025).

In 1731, Governor John Montgomerie adopted a new municipal charter ("Montgomerie Charter") that provided a portfolio, including City Hall, a market, docks, wharves, bridges, and plentiful public land that could be sold, leased, or otherwise improved, facilitating expansion (Steinberg, 2014). The Charter also included underwater land, allowing Manhattan's expansion into the bay, along with allowing laying streets, regulating markets, licensing trades, charging and collecting fees, declaring ordinances, setting up courts, and suing and being sued, among many other activities (Burrows & Wallace, 1999; Melosi, 2020). However, the city still had to follow English and provincial law and was not allowed to tax its residents, and its mayor, sheriff, coroner, and recorder still had to be appointed by the governor (Burrows & Wallace, 1999; Shorto, 2025).

New York's population increased from about 500 in 1645 to 32,000 in 1790 (Hassell, 1999), by which time it was part of the newly created United States. By comparison, Philadelphia had 28,522 residents in 1790 and Boston had 18,320 (Ballon, 2011c). In the early 1810s, New York City had about 100,000 residents, most of whom clustered downtown, south of Canal Street at the southern tip of Manhattan. Greenwich Village was the outpost to the north before settlement expanded northward (Bloomberg, 2011). At the same time, Beijing and London each had populations of about one million, and Paris had half a million (Ballon, 2011b, 2011c).

In 1811, New York City's governing and lawmaking Common Council bullishly forecast that the city would have about 400,000 people by 1860 (Ballon, 2011b, 2011c). Indeed, about 330,000 people resided in New York City in 1840, about 500,000 by 1850, about 813,000 by 1860, and about 2.5 million people in 1910 (Ballon, 2011c; see also Johnson, 1996).

In 1807, the New York state legislature appointed Founding Father Gouverneur Morris, New York State Surveyor General Simeon DeWitt, and major landowner John Rutherfurd to ordain the New York State Commissioners' Plan of 1811, which superimposed the previous Dutch, east–west-oriented grid with New York City's iconic Manhattan axis-oriented rectangular street grid (also called gridiron) with streets running from east to west north of 14th Street and south of 155th Street, along with 12 intersecting, parallel, 100-foot-wide avenues running from north to south in Midtown and Uptown Manhattan (Ballon, 2011a; Macaulay-Lewis, 2021; Spady, 2020; StreetEasy, 2018). Whereas some argue that the Plan of 1811 *followed* the local land market, others argue that it *led* the local land market, facilitating development and speculation and protecting the property values of powerful owners (Angotti, 2008; Azzarone, 2022). The local streets south of Houston Street had been developed before the Plan of 1811 was announced and thus did not follow that particular grid pattern (Macaulay-Lewis, 2021). These streets had names instead of numbers, such as Wall, Water, William, Beaver, Bridge, Broad, Mott, Mercer, Mulberry, Spruce, Cedar, and Pine Streets (Koeppel, 2015). Compared to Washington, DC and many major European cities, the Plan of 1811 has Broadway, the longest avenue in Manhattan as it only has one axial boulevard, running from the Bowery to the Battery, and diagonally crossing streets and avenues starting south of West 77th Street (Blake, 2020; Traub, 2011). The Plan also foresaw a few plazas or squares that offered open sightlines or vistas (Blake, 2020).

It took about 60 years for development to reach 155th Street, and later the gridiron was partially expanded to the Bronx. Brooklyn and Queens have several small gridirons, especially where large developments on superblocks were constructed, interior streets were closed, and public squares or parks were built (Ballon, 2011d; Lasner, 2016). While the Manhattan grid grew horizontally in the 19th century, it grew vertically in the 20th century (Ballon, 2011b).

The Plan of 1811 resulted in about 2,000 blocks, approximately 200 feet deep (north to south) and 250 to 920 feet wide (east to west), subdivided into 20 to 25 by 100-foot, standardized lots, with 155 numbered east–west cross streets that were each about 60 feet wide and 12 long main north–south avenues that were each about 100 feet wide (Bauer, 2020; Spady, 2020). The east–west cross streets facilitated access to the port facilities at the Hudson and East Rivers (Barr, 2016).

The Plan of 1811 had north–south avenues that were numbered, with the exception of four smaller A, B, C, and D avenues on the Lower East Side, Lexington Avenue (to honor the Battle of Lexington during the Revolutionary War), Madison Avenue (to commemorate the fourth president of the U.S.), and Park Avenue on the East Side (Rose-Redwood, 2011). In the 1880s and 1890s, New York City renamed several numbered avenues on the Upper West Side to make the area more appealing for property owners, including Eighth Avenue (relabeled Central Park West), Ninth Avenue (renamed Columbus Avenue), Tenth Avenue (relabeled Amsterdam Avenue), and Eleventh Avenue (renamed West End Avenue; Azzarone, 2022; Rose-Redwood, 2011). In the case of Harlem, north of Central Park, New York City renamed upper Sixth Avenue first Lenox Avenue in 1887 (for Scottish philanthropist Robert Lenox) and then Malcolm X Boulevard in 1987, Seventh Avenue to Adam Clayton Powell Jr. Boulevard in 1974, and Eighth Avenue to Frederick Douglass Boulevard in 1977 (Maurrasse, 2006). New York City also renamed some cross streets, including 106th Street for Duke Ellington in 1977, the four easternmost blocks of 116th Street for Luis Muñoz Marín in 1982 (Puerto Rico's first governor), 125th Street for Dr. Martin Luther King, Jr. in 1984, and 145th Street for A. Philip Randolph, an early labor and civil rights leader, in 2009 (Koeppel, 2015).

The Plan of 1811 has several advantages and disadvantages. In terms of advantages, it was simple to draw and theoretically easy to implement, extend, and supervise; it facilitated orderly land development and future growth; it used space effectively and efficiently; it enabled the commodification of and speculation with land through the sale and exchange of subdivided property lots; and it was pedestrian and bike friendly (Koeppel, 2015). In terms of disadvantages, the Plan of 1811 ignored natural topographical features such as hills, dales, swamps, springs, streams, ponds, forests, and meadows, as well as the efficiency of radials in terms of travel, resulting in some leveled hills and water quality and drainage challenges (Steinberg, 2014). It also did not provide alleyways, courtyards, or rear access streets, which were common in other older cities such as Philadelphia, as many future homebuyers favored bigger lots and did not have horse carriages and thus no need for rear stables, but this layout ultimately contributed to congested, overburdened streets without parking spaces and challenging waste collection and deliveries that had to occur from the street (Hamill, 2004). The Plan has long dimensions for each block facing north–south, causing the south facades to receive much sunlight and the north facades to receive natural light but no sunlight (Sorkin, 2009; Spady, 2020). It also did not provide space for public squares or parks, leading to sidewalks becoming the only places where people could spend time outdoors (Azzarone, 2022; Steinberg, 2014). The implementation of the Plan of 1811 also meant that previously designated lots were subdivided into slivers and that erected buildings were now overrun by measured, assessed, excavated, leveled, flattened, filled, graded, and eventually paved streets (Koeppel, 2015). The gridiron plan also did not include the 843-acre Central Park, which was first suggested in 1857 and designed by Frederick Law Olmsted and Calvert Vaux, following the modern English tradition of landscape architecture. Part of the park was built on the former site of Seneca Village, a community founded by members of the African Society for Mutual Relief and the African Methodist Episcopal Zion Church in 1825 on the principles of racial and personal advancement during the time of slavery (Sawadogo, 2022). Seneca Village was established between what is now West 82nd and West 85th Streets between Seventh and Eighth Avenues and had 225 residents, most of them African Americans, living in over 50 owner-occupied homes (Central Park Conservancy, n.d.; Sawadogo, 2022). However, they were displaced and dispersed in 1857 to make way for the construction of Central Park (Central Park Conservancy, n.d.; Sawadogo, 2022). Additionally, some have argued that the city's grid is monotonous, soulless, dull, and uninspiring (Steinberg, 2014).

The Plan of 1811 was contested by several displaced property owners, who requested that New York City modify the grid (Ballon, 2011d). Over time, some of these challenges were addressed by architects, traffic engineers, and housing reformers, including by creating avenues with different widths, as in the case of Madison and Lexington Avenues (each 80 feet wide), Park Avenue north of 4th Street (widened to 140 feet), and Lenox Avenue/Malcolm X Boulevard and Adam Clayton Powell Boulevard (each widened to 150 feet; Garvin, 2011). Some streets were eliminated to create superblocks that facilitated the development of major public works and institutions, including Columbia University, City College, the main branch of the New York Public Library, Pennsylvania Station, Grand Central Terminal, the United Nations Headquarters, and several major hospitals (Bender, 2002; Koeppel, 2015; Lasner, 2016; Macaulay-Lewis, 2021).

The Plan of 1811 popularized the common building practice of standard 25-foot-wide single lots but did not regulate it. This practice had evolved as early as the 1640s and was determined by the constraints of animal labor and hand machinery to utilize 18-foot-long sawn trees and, thus, the maximum spans of wooden floor joists without added internal columns (Koeppel, 2015). In the mid-19th century, as land prices increased, some developers and builders increased volume and efficiency by buying several adjacent lots, and sometimes even the entire perimeter, to construct multiple buildings within one block or by decreasing the width of houses from 25 feet (for upper-income households), to 18 to 20 feet (for middle-income households), to 12 to 14 feet (for lower-income households; Cromley, 1990; Plunz & Abu-Lughod, 1994).

Over the past two centuries, New York City's varied and resilient economy has gradually transitioned from a trade, to a blue-collar manufacturing, to a professional service and management, to a knowledge-based economy (Anheier, Lam, & Howard, 2013). New York City had federal and state government functions when it served as de facto capital from 1785 to 1788 and then de jure national capital from 1788 to 1790, followed by Philadelphia from 1790 to 1800, and then Washington, DC since 1800 (Asch & Musgrove, 2017; Rath, Foner, Duyvendak, & Reekum, 2014). New York City also served as state capital until 1797, when the city lost its state government function to Albany (Barr, 2016).

In the 18th, 19th, and early 20th centuries, New York City was not only a town of commerce and merchants but also a blue-collar manufacturing center, primarily focusing on sugar production and refining, garment manufacturing, iron production, and printing and publishing (Hood, 2017; Melosi, 2020; Rosenberg, 2014). Small manufacturers produced household goods such as bread, mustard, tobacco, patent leather items (including shoes, pocketbooks, and pencil cases), writing ink, tin ware, combs, and furniture (including iron chests and marble mantles) for wholesalers, auction houses, and consumers (Burrows & Wallace, 1999; Melosi,

2020). In 1910, about 40% of New York City's employees worked in manufacturing (Glaeser, 2005). New York City's employment in manufacturing peaked in 1947, while national employment in manufacturing peaked in 1956 (Zukin, 1989). From 1950 to 1975, employment in manufacturing in New York City decreased by about 50 to 60%, losing about 50,000 manufacturing jobs per year, especially in the garment and machinery (except electrical) industries, which was the largest absolute loss among all U.S. cities (Chin, 2005; Larson, 2013; Melosi, 2020). For example, there were between 963,000 and 991,000 jobs in manufacturing in late 1959, depending on the source (Woodsworth, 2016). However, there were less than 80,000 manufacturing jobs in New York City in 2010 (Berg, 2018).

Some of the factors that led to the loss of the city's manufacturing base was the interstate system (which decreased the advantage of a location in the central city and benefitted warehouses in the distant suburbs and trucking businesses), inadequate space in central cities that made expansions difficult, obsolescent multistory manufacturing buildings, insufficient investments for modernizing plants (and thus lower productivity), and relocations of entire companies to low-wage, non-unionized cities, regions, and countries (Sassen, 2001). While New York City's blue-collar employment in manufacturing decreased over time, white-collar employment in the finance, insurance, and real estate (FIRE) sector increased by 25%, in the professional services sector by 52%, and in the government sector by 53% from 1950 to 1975 (Hood, 2017; Larson, 2013). Service sector employment increased from 24% in 1970 to 42% in 2000, although service employment is bifurcated between services with relatively high wages with benefits, such as construction, and those with relatively low wages without benefits, such as retail, home health care, restaurants, personal services, food and apparel production, and building maintenance and security (Hum, 2014). While there has been a decrease in the proportion of people working in manufacturing and professional and business services, there has been an increase in the proportion of people working in the knowledge-based economy, as well as in the formal and informal low-income service ("gig") economy, often leading to housing affordability challenges for the latter group (Hood, 2017; Mele, 2007).

In the early 19th century, New York City was the center of sugar production, including refining, which prevents sugar crystals from coalescing in high temperatures; bleaching, which transforms brown sugarcane to white table sugar; and distilling, which converts sugar into rum (Burrows & Wallace, 1999; Wallace, 2017). Sugar production was the largest industry in New York City in 1810, consisting of more than one-third of the total manufactured value and benefiting from trade with the West Indies as well as economies of scale (Burrows & Wallace, 1999). In the late 19th century, New York City refined about half of the sugar consumed in the entire United States (Burrows & Wallace, 1999).

These manufacturing facilities were first clustered around port facilities on the Hudson River, the largest cluster during that time, and along the East River in Williamsburg (Zukin, 1991). For example, the American Sugar Refining Company built the Domino Sugar Refinery in Williamsburg in 1856, which was the largest sugar refining center in the world in the late 19th century (Baum, 2024; Burrows & Wallace, 1999; Wallace, 2017). After the building was destroyed by a fire, the company rebuilt the refinery in Brooklyn in 1882, where it operated until 2004 (Baum, 2024; Campo, 2013). In 2012, Two Trees Management bought the Domino Sugar Factory (Berg, 2018). Currently, the site is being redeveloped for mixed use, including community and commercial space, office space, (affordable) housing, and open space totaling over 2.2 million square feet (Baum, 2024; Campo, 2013). From 1870 to 1900, sugar production and refining was the second largest industry in New York City, making Brooklyn the sugar refining capital of the U.S. (Campo, 2013). Brooklyn was also the site of the Bulk Flour Center, constructed in 1964 as the largest distribution center for flour, serving many bakeries and macaroni factories in the region (Campo, 2013).

From the mid-19th century until the 1950s, New York City's garment industry was the nation's largest industrial cluster (Chin, 2005; Hood, 2017). In the early 19th century, the garment industry depended on the Cotton Triangle, in which bales of cotton grown and produced in the American South were shipped to England or New England and fabrics produced in and shipped from water-powered textile mills in England or New England were shipped to New York City (Burrows & Wallace, 1999). Initially, paid tailors and seamstresses, or unpaid wives and daughters, gradually turned fabrics into individually tailored clothing stitch by stitch. However, sailors did not have the time to wait on tailored clothes and most apprentices and bachelors did not have female family members in town or could not afford clothing (Hood, 2017). Thus, mass production of ready-to-wear (prêt-à-porter) clothes started in the 1820s (Burrows & Wallace, 1999). Thus, domestic garment making rapidly developed, transforming roughly cut and sewn materials into pants, shirts, and jackets (Chin, 2005).

In 1846 and 1850, Elias Howe and Isaac Singer both invented and perfected sewing machines, then pooled their rights, settling a patent dispute and further facilitating mass production of ready-to-wear clothing (Burrows & Wallace, 1999). In 1860, more than 80% of the nation's textiles entered the U.S. through New York City's port facilities (Glaeser, 2005). Demand for ready-to-wear clothing increased during the U.S. Civil War (Maffi, 1995). From 1860 to 1880, employment in the garment industry increased from about 29,000 to about 70,000 jobs (Mele, 2000). In 1880, New York City produced 40% of all ready-to-wear clothing in the U.S. (Chin, 2005).

While the textile mills needed large spaces, garment making could either occur in smaller factories in New York City's Garment District or at home (Glaeser, 2011). In 1890, almost 80% of the city's garment industry was located below 14th Street, where it produced a large share of the national output of women's and a smaller share of the national output of men's clothing (Foner, 2000; Wallace, 2017). In 1920, New York City's garment industry had about 165,000 workers (Chin, 2005).

Many workers in the garment industry were skilled in needlework and were parts of largely Eastern and Southern European ethnic and immigrant networks (Flood, 2010). Most factory owners in the garment industry, both retail and wholesale, were German (Foner, 2000). A great proportion of New York City's employment in manufacturing occurred in garment making, making up 30% in 1860, compared to 19% in 1900 and 27% in both 1940 and 1967, respectively (Currid, 2007). The concentration of the garment industry in the city made New York City a fashion design capital in the late 19th and 20th centuries (Chin, 2005). The concentration of the industry in New York City also gave rise to fashion magazines, such as *Harper's Bazaar* (established in 1867), *Vogue* (1892), and *Women's Wear Daily* (1910) and department stores such as Lord & Taylor (founded in 1826), Macy's (1858), Henri Bendel (1895–2019), and Bergdorf Goodman (1899). The fashion industry was also supported by the establishment of Pratt Institute (1888) and Parson's School of Design (1897), which helped inspire new clothing designs and led to further growth in the industry (Currid, 2007).

Until the 1950s, New York City's garment industry employed even more workers than the auto industry in Detroit (Glaeser, 2011). In the late 1960s and early 1970s, New York City's number of garment production facilities for ready-to-wear fashion rapidly declined due to competition from overseas (Zukin, 1991). These developments contributed to a vast absolute decrease in the number of jobs in the garment industry, from 354,000 in 1948, to 340,700 in 1950, to 267,000 in 1960, to about 150,000 in 1984 (Jonnes, 2002). Indeed, while apparel manufacturing in New York City made up about 33% of all employment in manufacturing in 1950, it was only almost 8% in 1996 (Chin, 2005).

Nevertheless, New York has remained a major center of global fashion, with many design studios, production facilities for both high-end (haute couture) and ready-to-wear fashion, showrooms, production facilities, and warehouses still in the Garment District and in (Manhattan's) Chinatown (Kantor, Lefèvre, Saito, Savitch, & Thornley, 2012). Indeed, about 11,000 (19%) of New York City's 60,000 garment workers were employed in (Manhattan's) Chinatown in 2000, while only about 800 workers were employed there in 2010, including in cut and sew shops (Hum, 2014). In sum, while mass production has decreased in the long run, small batch production has evolved over the past few decades. Indeed, since the late 1980s, some smaller garment production facilities have moved to immigrant neighborhoods in Brooklyn and Queens, escaping increasing commercial rents (Chin, 2005; Hum, 2014; McCormick, 2021). While much U.S. garment consumption is from Chinese imports, garments produced in and shipped from China need about six weeks to arrive in New York City. By contrast, garments, including small samples, small (test) runs, and replaced inventories, produced locally need less than two to three weeks (Chin, 2005; Hum, 2014).

New York City has also been called "the City of the Word," having served as the national center of printing and publishing activity and innovation for more than two centuries (Blake, 2020; Dyja, 2021, p. 60; Freeman, 2000; Rath et al., 2014). The American Company of Booksellers, a national trade organization founded in 1802, hosted book fairs attended by book sellers from all over the United States and also shipped copies inland (Burrows & Wallace, 1999). From 1860 to 1880, employment in printing and publishing increased from about 7,500 to more than 15,000 jobs (Mele, 2000). In the 1840s, the Pony Express, chartered locomotives, express steamships, carrier pigeons, and independently owned telegraph lines that connected New York, Washington, DC, Boston, and Albany facilitated the flow of information, followed by the transatlantic cable in the 1850s (Burrows & Wallace, 1999). Until 1886, the U.S. government refused to recognize foreign copyrights, so New York City's printing and publishing industry pirated copies from English authors, not paying royalties and benefiting from the popular transatlantic route to London (Burrows & Wallace, 1999).

From the 1830s to the 1900s, New York City's printing and publishing industry clustered in Newspaper Row at Chatham Street and Park Row (also known as Printing House Square) near City Hall, then clustered around Hudson Square west of SoHo (South of Houston), followed by the areas around Pennsylvania Station and the Post Office Complex (Macaulay-Lewis, 2021; Wallace, 2017). The *New York Herald Tribune* and *The New York Times* moved to Midtown in 1890 and 1904, respectively, the latter prompting the renaming of Longacre Square to Times Square (Macaulay-Lewis, 2021; Tippins, 2013; Wallace, 2017). Around the turn of the 20th century, writers, journalists, and poets patronized cafes, bars, and restaurants in Washington Square in Lower Manhattan (Bender, 2002; Macaulay-Lewis, 2021). New York City was also the home of national magazines, such as *Life* (established in 1883), *Time* (founded in 1923), *The New Yorker* (founded in 1925), *Esquire* (published since 1933), and *Look* (published from 1937 to 1971; Dyja, 2021; Greenberg, 2008). While the knowledge- and agglomeration-dependent publishing industry remained in Manhattan, the footloose printing industry dispersed to Brooklyn and eventually to the sunbelt and overseas after the mid-20th century (Lynch, n.d.).

In the early to mid-20th century, New York City's media industry evolved, innovated, and expanded rapidly (González, 2017). By the early 1920s, the Midtown office district had become firmly established (Blake, 2020; Johnson, 1996). Starting in the 1930s, many printing businesses downsized or shut down, while others left New York City for the suburbs due to high land prices, rents, and high labor costs (Flint, 2011). However, most publishing and media industries have remained prominent in New York City, as evidenced by the many literary agencies; book, magazine, and newspaper editorial offices; and large trade and university press publishers, including John Wiley & Sons, Inc. (founded in 1807), J. & J. Harper (founded in 1817) / Harper & Brothers (founded in 1833; now HarperCollins); Scribner's (founded in 1846); McGraw Hill (founded in 1888); Columbia University Press (founded in 1893); Doubleday (established in 1897); Grosset & Dunlap (founded in 1898); New York University Press (founded in 1916); and Random House (founded in 1927), among many others (Dyja, 2021; Rath et al., 2014; Wallace, 2017). Doubleday, Grosset & Dunlap, and Random House are now part of Penguin Random House, among other presses.

In the mid-1950s, the cost and difficulty of filming in New York City gradually increased, resulting in the film and television industry filming movies or movie scenes based in New York elsewhere (Caldwell, 2005). Thus, Mayor Lindsay tried to reinvigorate New York City's movie industry by establishing the Mayor's Office of Film, Theater, and Broadcasting (MOFTB), now the Mayor's Office of Media and Entertainment (MOME), in 1966 as a one-stop office to streamline filmmaking (City of New York, n.d.e). Over the past few decades, New York State and New York City have incentivized film and television production through several programs. For example, New York State passed the Film Production Tax Credit Program, which grants a 30% tax credit for qualified expenditures for eligible productions shot in New York City, in 1966 (City of New York, n.d.e). The New York State Post Production Tax Credit Program, passed in 2010, provides a 30% tax credit for qualified expenditures for eligible post-productions undertaken in New York City that did not qualify for the Film Production Tax Credit (Honegan, personal communication, September 7, 2021). New York City's

"Made in NY" Discount Card provides savings for eligible film and television producers in participating retail and service establishments (City of New York, n.d.e). New York City's "Made in NY" Marketing Credit program facilitates the marketing activities of film and television producers of films shot in New York City, such as printing bus shelter displays and subway cards, in return for using the "Made in NY" logo in end credits (City of New York, n.d.e). Outcomes included several dozen "asphalt jungle" and "New York exploitation" movies (i.e., crime thrillers, urban drama, blaxploitation, vigilante action, and horror movies) over the next few years (Greenberg, 2008). In sum, these activities sparked a movie renaissance, benefiting from New York City's improved image (Helmreich, 2016). Since the late 1910s and 1920s, New York City has also been home to many radio and television stations, including the Radio Corporation of America (RCA; founded in 1919); the American Broadcasting Company (ABC; established in 1927); the Columbia Broadcasting System (CBS; launched in 1928); the National Broadcasting Company (NBC; established in 1925 (radio) and 1939 (television)); and Bloomberg Television (launched in 1994; Moss, 2017). Radio City Music Hall (with almost 6,000 seats) opened in 1932, providing live entertainment and, until the late 1940s, CBS and NBC broadcasted live from the hall, not allowing recordings (Caldwell, 2005).

Currently, only about 2% of New York City's workforce works in manufacturing, most of it in the outer boroughs outside of Manhattan (Vitale, 2008). Nevertheless, in the mid-2000s, New York City established Industrial Business Zones (IBZs), which are "safe havens" that the city promised not to rezone, facilitating the retention and attraction of manufacturing and industrial companies. The city has subsidized the costs of companies moving to IBZs, often through a tax credit of $1,000 per employee, and up to $100,000 to defray relocation expenses (New York City Economic Development Corporation, n.d.b). Currently, there are 21 IBZs in four out of the five boroughs (except Manhattan; New York City Economic Development Corporation, n.d.b). From 1970 to 2000, New York City's so-called semi-skilled employment in professional and business services decreased from 60 to 45% (Currid, 2007). Indeed, since the mid-1950s, many manufacturing companies have moved from Lower Manhattan to either Midtown or suburban locations (Melosi, 2020; Moss, 2005; Sagalyn, 2016).

New York City's knowledge-based economy has been driven by financial and securities exchanges; national and international economic and political institutions (such as the United Nations and many other nongovernmental organizations, including Amnesty International); national and international banks and finance and insurance companies (centered around Wall Street); real estate, law, accounting, and media and advertising companies (clustered at Madison Avenue and around Times Square); management consulting firms; publishing firms (near Rockefeller Center); foundations (in Midtown Manhattan); arts and entertainment companies (around Broadway); the creative industry and global tastemakers and influencers, including fashion and design (centered around Seventh Avenue); high-end shopping and living (predominantly on Fifth Avenue and around Central Park); and wealth; as well as artists (residing on the Upper West Side, in Greenwich Village, the Financial District, in Chelsea, Clinton (also known as "Hell's Kitchen"), Midtown, the Upper East Side, Williamsburg, Greenpoint, Park Slope, Carroll Gardens, Brooklyn Heights, Fort Green, the Lower East Side, and (Manhattan's) Chinatown, among others (Anasi, 2012; Fainstein, 2010; Forman & Chaban, 2017; Morris, 2015; Wallace, 2017; Walters, 2014). Recently, some organizations in health care, technology, media and film, and higher education have moved to the outer boroughs (d'Almeida, 2018). The question remains whether these (re)locations are the beginning of a long-term trend.

FURTHER INFORMATION

Burrows, E. G., & Wallace, M. (1999). *Gotham: A history of New York City to 1898*. Oxford University Press.

Central Park Conservancy (n.d.). *Seneca Village site*. https://www.centralparknyc.org/locations/seneca-village-site

Macaulay-Lewis, E. (2021). *Antiquity in Gotham: The ancient architecture of New York City*. Fordham University Press.

Wallace, M. (2017). *Greater Gotham: A history of New York City from 1898 to 1919*. Oxford University Press.

DEMOGRAPHY AND IMMIGRATION

In the late 18th and early 19th centuries, New York City's population increased dramatically, going from about 18,000 in 1760, to 119,734 in 1810, to 152,026 in 1820, to 242,278 in 1830, to 313,000 in 1840, to 515,000 in 1850, and to just under 630,000 in 1855 (Steinberg, 2014). Since 1860, New York City has been the most populous city in the U.S., and much of the statistical population increase can be attributed to the incorporation of the five boroughs, as well as the regional and local economies being generally prosperous, immigration, and domestic migration, particularly of well-off households (Schwartz, 2019). In 1860, New York City's population reached 814,000, with 44% more residents than Philadelphia and about the same number as Paris (Steinberg, 2014). In 1870, 1880, and 1890, New York City had about 942,000, 1.2, and 1.5 million inhabitants, respectively—many more than the next three largest cities of Chicago, Philadelphia, and Brooklyn (Cromley, 1990; Wallace, 2017). New York City had more than 3.4 million residents in 1900, more than 4.7 million in 1910, more than 5.6 million in 1920, and more than 6.9 million in 1933 (Jonnes, 2002; Wallace, 2017). In 1940, 5.6% of the entire population of the U.S. lived in New York City (Glaeser, 2005).

New York City has been demographically more resilient than many other cities. For example, of the ten largest cities in 1930, almost all except New York City lost population from 1950 to 2000 (Glaeser, 2005). Indeed, New York City gained population over the past several decades, including from 1960 to 1970,

DOI: 10.1201/9781003624172-4

1980 to 1990 (almost 4%), 1990 to 2000 (13%), and 2000 to 2020 (from 8.008 to 8.8 million; U.S. Bureau of the Census, n.d.a). New York City only lost 1% of its population from 1950 to 1960, but it lost 10% from 1970 to 1980, partly triggered by abandonment, arson, and the fiscal crisis (Melosi, 2020). Interestingly, the population loss from 1970 to 1980 was the smallest of the ten largest cities of 1930 except Los Angeles, which gained during that decade (Glaeser, 2005). While New York City's population was 8.8 million as of April 2020, it was less than 8.3 million as of July 2023, partly due to the COVID-19 pandemic (U.S. Bureau of the Census, n.d.b).

For decades, New York City's population has been racially and ethnically diverse. For example, from 1990 to 2020, New York City's proportion of non-Hispanic Whites (1990: 43%, 2000: 35%, 2010: 33%, 2020: 31%) and Blacks/African Americans (1990: 29%, 2000: 27%, 2010: 26%, 2020: 23%) decreased, while its proportion of Hispanics/Latinos (1990: 24%, 2000: 27%, 2010: 29%, 2020: 28%) increased before recently slightly decreasing, and its proportion of Asians (1990: 7%, 2000: 10%, 2010: 13%, 2020: 15%) increased (Halle & Beveridge, 2013; U.S. Bureau of the Census, n.d.b). In the future, the proportion of non-Hispanic Whites will decrease, while the proportion of other racial and ethnic groups will increase. New York City's population has also been diverse in terms of religion. For example, New York City has had the largest Jewish community outside the state of Israel (Mollenkopf & Sonenshein, 2013).

For centuries, the United States and New York City have been destinations for ambitious migrants and immigrants who have pursued economic opportunity or have fled persecution (or both) and have become an integral part of the city (Rath et al., 2014). From 1820 to 1839, more than 667,000 immigrants arrived in the U.S., less than 90,000 per year (Barr, 2016). The annual number of immigrant arrivals from both 1841 to 1848 and 1855 to 1865 was less than 250,000, while it was higher than 250,000 from 1849 to 1854 (Cromley, 1990). In 1854, there were 428,000 immigrants total (Burrows & Wallace, 1999). After the U.S. Civil War, the annual number of immigrants increased again. In 1870, there were 400,000, and there were more than 450,000 immigrants who came to the U.S. in 1880, 1890, and 1900 (Flood, 2010).

Between 1903 and 1914, almost 12 million immigrants in total arrived, most of whom were from Europe and Russia and fueled by the decrease in costs for transatlantic passage (Barr, 2016). After 1914, numbers rapidly decreased, impacted by World War I, then briefly spiked around 1920, before decreasing again after the Immigration (Johnson-Reed) Act of 1924 became effective, which limited the annual number of immigrants from any country to 2% of the number who had arrived in 1890 (thus favoring Northern and Western Europeans, restricting Southern and Eastern Europeans, and near-banning Caribbeans, Africans, and Asians; Blake, 2020; Foner, 2013). Numbers also decreased due to the Chinese Exclusion Act, previously passed in 1882, the Great Depression, and World War II (Gurock, 2019). The Immigration Act of 1924 disproportionately affected New York City, as about 75% of its residents were either foreign born or had foreign-born ancestors (Melosi, 2020).

In 1965, Congress passed the Immigration and Nationality (Hart–Cellar) Act, which ended the national origins formula, placing immigrants from all nations on equal footing and favoring family unifications and immigrants with professional skills (Gurock, 2019). Then, Congress passed the Immigration and Reform Control Act (IRCA) of 1986, which legalized most undocumented immigrants who had arrived before January 1, 1982 while also making it illegal for employers to knowingly hire undocumented immigrants (Hum, 2014). Congress then passed the Immigration Act of 1990, which allowed for an increased number of visas based on family preferences compared to the number of visas based on employment, although an investor category was added (Hum, 2014).

For much of the 20th century, New York City had a proportion of immigrants of more than 20% (Foner, 2013). Indeed, from 1820 to 1859, about 75% of all immigrants entering the U.S. (i.e., half a million total from 1820 to 1839 and more than four million total from 1840 to 1859) arrived in New York, making it the gateway for new arrivals (Blake, 2020; Vickerman, 2013). However, the proportion of immigrants settling in New York City has varied over the past decades and centuries. It increased from 6% (1806), to 10% (1819), to over 20% (1825), and peaked at almost 50% (1870), but then it decreased to 37% (1900), increased to 41% (1910), and then decreased to 36% (1920), 34% (1930), 29% (1940), 24% (1950),

20% (1960), and 18% (1970; Foner, 2013). However, the proportion of immigrants settling in New York City has since continuously increased, from 24% (1980), to 28% (1990), to 36% (2000), and to 38% (2023; City of New York, 2023; Foner, 2013). From 1900 to 1950, New York City's proportion of all immigrants in the entire nation steadily increased from 12% (1900) to 18% (1940), before steadily decreasing to 8% (2010; Foner, 2013).

Immigrants have entered the United States due to such so-called push factors as people escaping past, present, or future religious or civic persecution, conflicts, violence, or poverty and such so-called pull factors as people (re)joining family members, friends, or neighbors, pursuing an education, obtaining a job, or starting or continuing a career to achieve or maintain middle-class status (Venkatesh, 2013; Wilkerson, 2010). While many immigrants enter the United States legally, others enter it non-legally or overstay their visas (Berg, 2018). There were about 467,000 undocumented immigrants in New York City, based on 2019 data, the most recent available data as of this writing (City of New York, 2024).

In April 2022, Texas Governor Greg Abbott launched Operation Lone Star, aiming "to secure the border; stop the smuggling of drugs, weapons, and people into Texas; and prevent, detect, and interdict transnational criminal activity between ports of entry" (Office of the Texas Governor, 2024, n.p.). As of January 2024, Texas has bused more than 100,000 undocumented immigrants to Democratic-led "sanctuary cities," including over 37,000 to New York City (since August 2022), over 30,000 to Chicago (also since August 2022), over 15,000 to Denver ("since May 18," year not provided), and over 12,000 to Washington, DC (since April 2022), among other cities (Garcia, 2024; Office of the Texas Governor, 2024, n.p.). As of December 2023, New York City had received more than 161,000 immigrants, with more than 68,000 remaining in town (Befferman, 2023). Thus, New York City Mayor Eric Adams issued an executive order mandating that bus drivers departing from Texas announce their arrival at least 32 hours in advance and arrive only between 8:30 am and noon on weekdays (Befferman, 2023). In January 2024, New York City filed a lawsuit against 17 bus and transportation companies that had contracted with the State of Texas to transport undocumented immigrants to New York City, seeking $708 million in damages (Garcia, 2024).

In sum, the influx of undocumented immigrants has challenged already strained local support systems, with the national and state political situations in flux as of this writing.

Many immigrants have benefitted from networks of voluntary mutual aid societies that have provided charitable support and opportunities for social engagement with compatriots since the late 19th century (Bagchee, 2018; Freeman, 2000). Examples of these mutual aid societies include the German Society of the City of New York (active from 1784 to 1984) and the still operating Order Sons of Italy in America (established in Little Italy in 1905, now the Order Sons and Daughters of Italy in America; Order Sons and Daughters of Italy in America, n.d.; Smithsonian Institution, n.d.; Ziegler-McPherson, 2022). Over time, there have been many conflicts between longtime residents and immigrants, such as Black/ African American boycotts of Korean stores in the 1980s and 1990s or conflicts in Flushing between non-Hispanic Whites and Chinese immigrants in the 1990s (Eng, 2022; Foner, 2013).

In the 19th and early 20th centuries, immigrants to the U.S. arrived at five points of entry: New York, Boston, Baltimore, Philadelphia, and New Orleans, with New York City the most commonly used port (Ballon, 2011c). From 1855 to 1890, the Castle Garden Emigrant Landing Depot and then, from 1892 to 1924, Ellis Island served as the formal entry points for most immigrants to the U.S., processing about eight million and 12 million entries, respectively (Rath et al., 2014; Ziegler-McPherson, 2022). Many immigrants remained in New York City because its manufacturing industry provided job opportunities that matched their skill sets, especially in the garment industry, but also because many lacked the resources to move somewhere else due to relatively high domestic transportation costs (Barr, 2016). Most low-income immigrants worked manual jobs, such as in the garment industry, where about 95% of workers were foreign-born (Burrows & Wallace, 1999). In 1855, about 55 and 35% of workers in this industry were German and Irish, respectively (Burrows & Wallace, 1999; Melosi, 2020). Many Irish immigrants worked in construction, at the port docks as stevedores, dock workers, or shipbuilders, or in warehouses and factories (Mele, 2000). German immigrants typically worked in the trades, in warehouses, and in construction (Shepard & Noonan, 2018; Ziegler-McPherson, 2022).

Many low- and middle-income immigrants established peddling carts at street corners and small grocery stores in immigrant neighborhoods when there was a breakdown of the city's public market system (Burrows & Wallace, 1999). For example, many Irish sold vegetables, iron, brass, copper, and second-hand goods or opened porter houses or taverns; many Germans sold dry goods and small manufactured items and worked as butchers, brewers, tobacconists, cigar makers, tailors, and piano builders (Wallace, 2017; Ziegler-McPherson, 2022). Some English, Scottish, Welsh, and Germans worked as printers (Burrows & Wallace, 1999).

In the 18th century, the Dutch were the major immigrant group (Jonnes, 2002). In the 19th century, there were four major immigrant groups to the U.S.: the Irish and the Germans, who arrived in the mid-19th century, and Russians/Eastern Europeans and Italians, who arrived in the late 19th century (Blake, 2020; Cohen, 2019; Melosi, 2020). From 1840 to 1859, 40% of immigrants were Irish, 32% were German, and 16% were English (Foner, 2013). By 1880, there were about 550,000 German immigrants and their U.S.-born children in New York City, making up about half of its 1.2 million residents (Ziegler-McPherson, 2022). In 1900, almost 45% of foreign-born residents in Manhattan were Irish or German, while almost 30% were Italian or from the Russian empire (including Ukraine, most of Poland, Lithuania, and Latvia; Blake, 2020; Foner, 2014; Sharman, 2006). Currently, an estimated 55% of New York City's population is either first- or second-generation immigrants (Foner, 2014).

Whereas four primarily European groups came to New York City in the 19th century, many different groups from Asia, Latin America, and the Caribbean arrived in the 21st century, facilitated by the Hart–Celler Act of 1965 (Zhou, 2013). Between the early 1950s and the mid-1980s, many Koreans moved to the U.S., triggered by the Korean War (1950–1953) and political instability in the 1960s, 1970s, and early 1980s (Howe, 2010). In the early 1970s, people from the Soviet Union were allowed to emigrate, followed by people from China in the late 1970s (Foner, 2013).

In 1970, 64% of immigrants in New York City were from Europe (i.e., Italy, Poland, the (then) USSR, Germany, and Ireland; Lobo & Salvo, 2013). In 2010, about one-third of immigrants were from Latin America (i.e., the Dominican Republic,

Mexico, and Ecuador; Lobo & Salvo, 2013). In the late 20th and early 21st centuries, New York City's immigrant diversity became unique among U.S. cities, as there are no single or multiple dominant origin countries, although there are many immigrants who hail from the Caribbean (Foner, 2013). In 2022, Dominicans made up about 13% of all immigrants in New York City, followed by the Chinese (including those from Taiwan and Hong Kong; 12%), Mexicans (5.4%), Jamaicans (almost 5%), and Guyanans (4.6%; City of New York, 2023). Other groups hailed from Ecuador, Bangladesh, Haiti, Colombia, and Trinidad and Tobago (City of New York, 2023).

Over the past several decades, many Asian and European groups arriving in New York City have had among the highest levels of education, whereas many Latin American and Hispanic and Caribbean groups have had among the lowest (Lobo & Salvo, 2013). Immigrants own about 90% of dry cleaners and laundries, 84% of small grocery stores, and 70% of beauty salons in New York City (Foner, 2013). New York City has experienced an ethnic division of labor because of job referrals among networks, cultural preferences, skills, and training (Foner, 2013). For example, Korean immigrants took over many delicatessens, previously run by Greeks and Italians, most dry-cleaning businesses, previously managed by the Chinese, many nail salons, previously run by African Americans, and some bodegas, previously owned by Dominicans (Eng, 2022; Min, 2013). Most Korean owners of corner stores added delicatessen counters, salad bars, and flower sections to compete against emerging chain megastores (Dyja, 2021). Many cab and passenger van drivers hail from South Asia, in particular Pakistan; most health-care workers and nursing aides are from Jamaica, Haiti, and the Caribbean; most street vendors and many small business owners are from India or West Africa; many restaurant workers are from China and many food preparers are from Mexico (Foner, 2013; Hodges, 2020).

New York City has had a higher number and proportion of immigrants and children and grandchildren of immigrants than any other major city in the U.S. (Foner, 2013). In the 19th century, most immigrant groups arrived in New York City and initially moved to ethnic neighborhoods (also called "enclaves"), like Five Points, with relatively high concentrations of their compatriots or family members speaking their native languages, making the transition to the New World easier (Cromley, 1990; Spady, 2020). Before the 1920s, many of the Irish, Eastern Europeans, and Italians first arrived in Manhattan and then moved to the Bronx (Helmreich, 2023). The Irish clustered in Mott Haven, Melrose, and Highbridge; the Eastern Europeans concentrated in Hunt's Point, West Farms, and East Tremont; and the Italians resided in Morrisania and Beltmont (Jonnes, 2002). After a few years or decades, many groups decentralized to Brooklyn or other outer boroughs (Barr, 2016; Ziegler-McPherson, 2022). In 2022, Queens (almost 37%) and Brooklyn (about 27%) had the highest concentration of immigrants, followed by the Bronx (17.1%), Manhattan (14.9%), and Staten Island (3.9%; City of New York, 2023).

FURTHER INFORMATION

City of New York. (2024). *Facts, not fear: How welcoming immigrants benefits New York City.* https://comptroller.nyc.gov/reports/facts-not-fear-how-welcoming-immigrants-benefits-new-york-city/#:~:text=Approximately%20476%2C000%20undocumented%20immigrants%20lived,compared%20to%20504%2C000%20in%202018.

Foner, N. (Ed.). (2013). *One out of three: Immigrant New York in the twenty-first century.* Columbia University Press.

U.S. Bureau of the Census (n.d.b). Quick facts: New York City, New York. https://www.census.gov/quickfacts/fact/table/newyorkcitynewyork/PST045224

Ziegler-McPherson, C. A. (2022). *The great disappearing act: Germans in New York City, 1880–1930.* Rutgers University Press.

ECONOMY

Since the mid-20th century, global and major cities, among them New York, London, and Tokyo, have been competing with each other (Fainstein, 2001; Gladstone & Fainstein, 2013; Molotch, 1976). The competition among global and major cities may be illustrated through rankings (Sassen, 2001). For example, the Globalization and World Cities Research Network (GaWC) regularly analyzes office networks of 175 advanced producer service firms in 707 major cities (Globalization and World Cities Research Network, 2024). In 2024, GaWC differentiated among alpha ++, alpha +, alpha, and alpha −, beta-level cities, gamma-level cities, and cities with sufficiency of services (Globalization and World Cities Research Network, 2024). New York City and London rank at the very top and have the alpha ++ status (Globalization and World Cities Research Network, 2024).

Global and major cities have served three major roles (Gladstone & Fainstein, 2013). First, they are command and control centers in the international economy, exemplified by the number of international companies focusing on financial, legal, marketing, advertisement, and other specialized services, many of them operating from headquarters in glass and steel skyscrapers built in the International Style (Bender, 2002; Gladstone & Fainstein, 2013). Second, they serve as hubs of global culture and, third, they function as centers of producer services (Gladstone & Fainstein, 2013).

New York City's employment by industry may be summarized by location quotients (LQs), which compare the concentration of

DOI: 10.1201/9781003624172-5

a particular industry with the national concentration of the entire industry, (i.e., the numerator displays the ratio of employment in a specific industry divided by the total employment in the city and the denominator contains the ratio of employment in the industry in the nation divided by the total employment in the nation; Gladstone & Fainstein, 2013). An LQ greater than 1.0 means that the average local employment share is higher than the average national employment share in a certain industry (Gladstone & Fainstein, 2013). In the second quarter of 2024, the occupations in the private sector with the highest employment LQs in Manhattan (New York County) were information (4.17), financial activities (2.99), professional and business services (1.67), and general services (1.25; U.S. Bureau of Labor Statistics, n.d.).

There are multiple reasons for New York City's premier status among global and major cities. The city enjoys an enormous concentration of capital and has been called the "capital of capital," the "capital of the financial and business worlds," and the "economic capital of the world," as evidenced by Wall Street and its New York Stock Exchange (NYSE), which was established in 1792 and based on capital extracted from slavery and Southern agriculture (Feagin, 2016; Morris, 2015). As of this writing, New York City is home to 41 Fortune 500 companies, the highest number of all major cities in the entire United States, including JP Morgan Chase, Verizon Communications, and Citigroup (Burleigh, 2024; City of New York, 2019; Nave, n.d.; The Center Square, 2020). Also, New York City is the home of 110 Forbes-listed billionaires, including Michael Bloomberg, Julia Koch and family, and Jim Simons; the highest number of high-net-worth individuals (HNWIs) in the nation; and a high number of international expatriates (Bell & de-Shalit, 2011, p. 249, p. 260; Fitch, 1993, p. 13; Grosser, 2024).

Over centuries, many of New York City's companies have influenced local, state, and national policymakers, such as by negotiating property tax exemptions (Barr, 2016). Examples of real estate developers include the LeFrak family (builders of LeFrak City in Queens), Fred Trump (builder of Trump Village, Shore Haven, and Beach Haven, all in Brooklyn), the Tishman family (one of the founding partners of Tishman Speyer, which bought Stuyvesant Town in 2006 and ceded ownership in 2010), and the Durst

Organization (builders of One World Trade Center in Manhattan; The Durst Organization, n.d.; Larson, 2017; LeFrak, n.d.).

New York City has also been called the nation's and possibly the globe's "capital of culture," with many cultural and tourist attractions, partly due to the historic support of philanthropists, such as Cornelius Vanderbilt, Jay Gould, and J. P. Morgan; foundations, such as the Ford Foundation, the Jewish Communal Fund, the Andrew W. Mellon Foundation, the New York Community Trust, and the JPMorgan Chase Foundation (The Grantsmanship Center, n.d.). Philanthropists not only provided money but also donated or loaned their personal art collections to museums (Zukin, 1995). In 1870, the New York State Legislature granted New York City's Metropolitan Museum of Art ("the Met") an Act of Incorporation, enabling it to open in 1872 (Zukin, 1995). In the 1920s and 1930s, New York City's arts establishment founded the Museum of Modern Art (MoMA; 1929), the Whitney Museum (1931), and the Solomon R. Guggenheim Museum (1937; Bender, 2002; Currid, 2007). From 1935 to 1943, the Works Progress Administration (WPA) provided job opportunities to jobless people in the entire nation, including about 700,000 New Yorkers in construction, white-collar professions, and the arts (Gregory, 1998). In New York City, WPA-supported workers built LaGuardia airport and rebuilt and renovated public libraries and public parks, roadways, and sewers (Gregory, 1998). The WPA also tasked artists with creating public art and murals and encouraged them to organize themselves in unions or work-related groups through formal collaborations and informal networking, which benefitted about 2,000 artists in New York City, or almost 50% of about 5,000 supported artists nationwide, including Arshille Gorky, Adolph Gottlieb, Willem de Kooning, Jackson Pollock, and Mark Rothko (Currid, 2007). One of these groups was the Tenth Street School of Abstract Expressionists, which later became known as the New York School (Zukin, 1989).

In the mid- and late 20th century, Greenwich Village was the home of bohemian, abstract expressionism (1940s), pop art (mid- to late 1950s), neo-Dada (1960s), and postmodernist artists (e.g., Keith Haring, Jasper Johns, Roy Lichtenstein, Robert Rauschenberg, and Andy Warhol; Dyja, 2021). There were beat writers in the 1960s (e.g., William Burroughs, Alan

Ginsberg, and Jack Kerouac) and musicians who played mambo (late 1930s), bebop (1940s), reggae (1960s), new wave (1970s), hip hop or rap (early 1970s), punk (mid-1970s), and disco (late 1970s and early 1980s) (Helmreich, 2023; Phillips-Fein, 2017; Vickerman, 2013). The art movement reinvigorated many challenged neighborhoods, which eventually gentrified (Mele, 2000). Some argue that in the 2000s, New York City's creative industry (labeled the "Warhol economy") has a relatively high number of employees, even more than the FIRE industry (Currid, 2007; Morris, 2015). In the 20th century, New York City was also center of the feminist and gay movements, possibly stimulated by the many European emigres who brought both intellectual and artistic capital with them (Kaiser, 2019).

Over the past decades, New York City has experienced many economic peaks and valleys triggered by national and regional recessions, which lasted several months and sometimes several years. As stated by Lobo and Salvo (2013, p. 35), "[t]he success of any great city lies in its capacity to reinvent itself over time. [...]. The energy unleashed by a city continuously remaking itself demographically [...] allows it to reinvent itself socially, culturally, and economically." Compared to other major cities, New York City's economy has been relatively resilient and mostly prosperous. Indeed, from the mid-1940s to the mid-1960s, New York City was the nation's flagship city, serving as the center of capital, FIRE, entertainment, manufacturing, and shipping (Galster, 2012). New York City even fared somewhat well after the stock market crash on October 19, 1987 ("Black Monday"), which caused the global economy to crash (Manshel, 2020). Compared to many other major U.S. cities, New York City "only" experienced one decade-long local economic decline in the 1970s, as evidenced by increasing welfare needs, crime, substance use in public, deteriorating public schools, vandalized parks, and widespread graffiti (Kinder, 2016; Kirshner, 2019; Medoff & Sklar, 1994).

Since the 1970s, and especially since the early 1980s, many cities have pursued neoliberal and entrepreneuralist approaches, focusing on global and domestic inter-urban competition and local civic boosterism through economic development facilitated by the business establishment and partnerships, including circulating and attracting capital; attracting global corporate headquarters and highly skilled workers; investing in advanced transportation and communication infrastructure; redeveloping downtowns, commercial office space, and tourism; offering business services; and renaming neighborhoods, all facilitated by lowered corporate taxes (Florida, 2002; Mallach & Swanstrom, 2023; Molotch, 1976). While many cities have focused on high-end jobs, the number of low-end jobs in the service sector to serve full-time workers has also increased, including in restaurants, retail, child and home care, security, and dry-cleaning facilities, among others (Kallick, 2013). These low-end jobs, many of them with relatively low wages and few or no benefits, replaced jobs in manufacturing, which typically paid relatively high wages and had many benefits because of the cumulative effects of union negotiations over decades (Sassen, 2001). In turn, some cities may focus less on supporting small businesses; labor, social, and environmental equity; manufacturing; and the transportation of physical goods, partially caused by well-funded anti-union efforts and lobbying, leading to increased and increasing polarization (Kantor et al., 2012). Since this era, luxury housing developers have become more active (Kuttner, 2021).

The 1970s were a decade "when the old American dream fell apart, when unemployment and inflation replaced the steady prosperity of the postwar years and the international supremacy of the United States ceased to be something to take for granted" (Phillips-Fein, 2017, p. 4). From 1975 to 1978, New York City experienced the largest citywide municipal fiscal crisis in the history of the United States (Bender, 2002). The severe impacts of this crisis lasted about a decade and have continued to touch almost all New Yorkers, especially low-income people who depended on public services (Freeman, 2000; Phillips-Fein, 2017). The crisis was partially triggered by international, national, and local challenges.

In terms of international challenges, the international oil price crisis in 1973 and 1974 was triggered by an oil embargo by the Organization of Petroleum Exporting Countries (OPEC) against the U.S. and other countries that had supported Israel in the Yom Kippur War (Flood, 2010). It not only affected the supporting countries but also so-called developing countries, as they were unable to pay back loans held by international organizations or New York-based banks, affecting their liquidity (Soffer, 2010). In terms of national challenges, there was long-term high inflation and increasing unemployment (and thus stagflation), federal retrenchment in urban areas and preference for suburban development, long-term governance challenges, short-term stagnant growth, and the rising costs of the Vietnam War (Kallick, 2013).

In terms of local economic, fiscal, infrastructure, and political challenges, debt-financed development of newly built, high-end office space gradually caused land values to increase while the values of some existing residential and commercial properties decreased. In addition, local employment in the manufacturing industry decreased; local support from the federal and state sectors decreased while employment in the local public sector increased due to powerful union negotiations; inter-urban competition increased; and the regional and local infrastructure continued to decay (Flood, 2010; Fuchs, 1992; Phillips-Fein, 2017). In addition, the Metropolitan Transportation Authority (MTA) lost about half of its riders (Ocejo, 2014). Many local politicians dependant on local interest groups to create winning electoral coalitions were unable to meet or deflect their demands (Fuchs, 1992).

These challenges contributed to a dramatic loss of almost 1 million residents in New York City (slightly less than 10%) from 1970 to 1980 (Dyja, 2021). There was also a substantial drop in visitors, all translating into decreased tax revenue (Soffer, 2010). Furthermore, there was a decrease in the number of Fortune 500 companies headquartered in New York City, from 139 in 1958, to 128 in 1966, to 84 in 1976, and to 53 in 1986. Competing companies merged and acquired other corporations, were no longer on the Fortune 500 list, or moved their headquarters, such as to the suburbs of Westchester County or Bergen County, New Jersey, the Sunbelt, or overseas (Matsumoto, 2018). However, six new Fortune 500 firms relocated to New York City between 1970 and 1976, and the number of foreign banks with local offices increased from 46 to 84 (Osman, 2011).

During the 1960s and 1970s, there had been a long-term increase in salaries and benefits for public employees, and an increased number of low-income people who received higher welfare, Medicaid, and other benefits, some of which were matched by the city (Fitch, 1993; Fuchs, 1992; Soffer, 2010). Over the past centuries and decades, the city had deeply invested in its residents, providing an unheard-of range of services that resulted in a symbiotic relationship between the city's blue-collar economy and its generous local welfare state (Freeman, 2000).

For example, New York City provided 24 municipal hospitals, dozens of neighborhood primary care and pediatric clinics, a network of municipal colleges, an extensive continuing education program, many neighborhood daycare centers for low-income parents, and treatment clinics for drug users, among many other facilities (Phillips-Fein, 2017). However, over time there were increased municipal housing and education expenditures amid annual budget shortfalls, a decreasing tax reserve, and long-term declining and then frozen bond and credit ratings, partially triggered by massive, ineffective, expensive, unsustainable, and questionable short-term municipal borrowing for long-term projects (instead of increasing taxes; Melosi, 2020; Phillips-Fein, 2017).

New York City is required to balance its annual budget, not leaving a deficit or surplus like the federal government (Flood, 2010). While cities issue long-term general obligation bonds to finance capital improvements, which are subject to voter oversight or approval, New York City is allowed to cover budget shortfalls by issuing tax-exempt or low-interest municipal bonds that do not require voter oversight or approval or passing or increasing taxes (Phillips-Fein, 2017). The city is also required to make budget forecasts, updated quarterly, with four-year projections (Sweeting & Dinneen, 2013). In the late 1960s and early 1970s, New York City had forecasted overly optimistic future revenues, underestimating its obligations, underfunding municipal pensions, rerouting funds obtained for capital to operating expenditures, and issuing checks late (Fuchs, 1992; Phillips-Fein, 2017; Sweeting & Dinneen, 2013). In spring 1974, almost 28% of all tax-exempt bonds and notes in the entire U.S. were originated in New York City (Phillips-Fein, 2017).

A municipality's fiscal condition may be assessed in terms of the amount of its outstanding debts or in terms of its per capita common function debt, among other measures (Fuchs, 1992). In terms of outstanding debts, New York City had $11.4 billion in outstanding debts in spring 1975, including almost $6 billion in short-term debt, and thus needed to roll over about $750 million in short-term notes each month to service long-term debt, paying higher interest rates (Fuchs, 1992; Sharman, 2006). Another measure is per capita common function debt. Municipal function expenditures, which are differentiated based on common versus non-common expenditures, are based on political decisions. Common municipal function expenditures include investments in general control, financial administration, general government building, police and fire protection, and sanitation and sewers, as well as highways, parks, and recreation (Fuchs, 1992). Non-common function expenditures include investments in health, hospitals, utilities, corrections, public welfare, education, and libraries, as well as housing and neighborhoods (Fuchs, 1992). In the 1960s and 1970s, New York City provided many more non-common functions than other cities. Thus, Fuchs (1992, p. 36) argues that if New York City had provided fewer non-common functions, "its fiscal condition would have remained relatively stable."

In April 1975, the City was ultimately unable to pay its operating expenses, including payroll (Sweeting & Dinneen, 2013). New York City's fiscal crisis led to banks deciding to first sell off all New York City short-term bonds in early 1975, anticipating default, and then deciding to stop selling these bonds and blocking Mayor Beame's efforts to underwrite future municipal bonds (Freeman, 2000; Fuchs, 1992; Soffer, 2010). These activities caused the municipal bond market to freeze until 1976, requiring the city to use about one-third of its expenses for debt service in 1977 and decreasing bond ratings and resources for economic development for many years (Dyja, 2021; Holtzman, 2021). International and national pressure increased as experts realized that the city's potential bankruptcy could negatively impact the national economy and the U.S. dollar, perhaps even bolstering the Soviet Union (Phillips-Fein, 2011). Since President Ford was unwilling to provide a federal bailout for New York City's debts, as (supposedly) exemplified in the *Daily News* headline of "FORD TO CITY: DROP DEAD," New York City took on a federal loan, to be repaid with high interest, and narrowly escaped bankruptcy. Ultimately, these loans were not sustainable (Fuchs, 1992; Phillips-Fein, 2017).

New York City lost its fiscal autonomy for several years and became more dependent on the State. For example, in June 1975, New York State passed the New York State Financial Emergency Act (FEA) and created supra-governmental independent emergency institutions, such as the Municipal Assistance Corporation

(MAC), a temporary public-benefit corporation headed by leaders in the financial industry appointed by the governor (Fainstein, 2001; Koch, 1985). MAC assisted the city in meeting its debt obligations by refinancing short-term with longer-term municipal bonds backed by a first lien of the municipal stock transfer tax and sales tax receipts, guiding the city towards a balanced budget (Berg, 2018; Phillips-Fein, 2017). However, selling these refinanced bonds was challenging, as the cost of borrowing was high (Soffer, 2010). New York City took on federal loans, an $800 million advance from the state, and support from investors, holders of municipal bonds, property developers, and CEOs of large financial institutions and corporations, who agreed to renew loans, lower interest rates, and extend repayment times (Greenberg, 2008, p. 128; Phillips-Fein, 2017). For example, New York City's pension fund and other municipal unions bought MAC's refinanced municipal bonds for $2.5 billion over a 2.5-year period to bail out private bondholders, forgoing interest payments in exchange for a seat at the negotiation table when the municipal budget was adjusted (Freeman, 2000; Phillips-Fein, 2017; Sweeting & Dinneen, 2013).

In September 1975, New York State established the Emergency Financial Control Board (EFCB), which consisted of seven members overseen by New York State, including the governor, the mayor, the state and city comptrollers, and three executives of the local business establishment, essentially placing the city in state receivership (Fainstein, 2001; Fuchs, 1992; Soffer, 2010). In 1975/1976, the EFCB began running New York City's finances as a shadow government, developing a financial plan for a balanced budget (Dyja, 2021). The EFCB was allowed to audit any financial aspect and control municipal revenues and expenditures through the EFCB Fund (Berg, 2018). In 1977, President Jimmy Carter decided against declaring New York City a disaster area, preventing the city from qualifying for federal assistance (Soffer, 2010).

In 1978, New York state eliminated the term "emergency" from the EFCB, now calling it either the New York State Financial Control Board (NYSFCB) or the Financial Control Board (FCB) (Fuchs, 1992; Phillips-Fein, 2017). In 1979, the Board began allowing New York City to offer bonds again, and it was able to balance its budget in fiscal year 1981 (Fuchs, 1992). Until 1983, when the economy had recovered and the emergency was declared to be over, the FCB continued to supervise and further implement New York City's local government finances on behalf of municipal bondholders, eliminate the stock exchange tax, set the real estate tax at a record low, reduce the personal income tax, and approve or disapprove labor contracts, and also oversaw the city's budgeting process in case the city was unable to balance its budget (Busà, 2017). In 1986, the FCB stopped formally approving New York City's financial plans (Fuchs, 1992; Phillips-Fein, 2017). However, the FCB/NYSFCB was still allowed to potentially overtake New York City's budgeting process in case the city was unable to balance its budget until 2008 (Sweeting & Dinneen, 2013). In 1989, the City of New York established the Independent Budget Office (IBO), a publicly funded nonpartisan agency to evaluate the mayor's budget proposals and revenue estimates (Independent Budget Office of the City of New York, n.d.).

The MAC and the EFCB also suggested many local austerity measures (Roberts, 2006). For example, New York City decreased city employment by about 69,000 employees (20%) until 1978, and either reduced or only nominally increased wages between June 1975 and April 1976 (Phillips-Fein, 2017; Soffer, 2010). It also reduced the number of police officers and teachers by 6,000 each and decreased the city's number of firefighters by about 2,500, especially in low-income neighborhoods (Fuchs, 1992; Sweeting & Dinneen, 2013; Thabit, 2003).

New York City raised taxes; decreased capital spending by almost 75%; nearly stopped maintaining, repairing, and replacing municipal facilities; reduced the number of sanitation workers; scaled or closed social programs; reduced salaries of government employees; reduced or eliminated welfare payments (hitting people of color especially hard); reduced or deinstitutionalized (mental) healthcare services (a growing national trend); asked homeowners to pay property taxes early in return for a discount; and asked local unions to agree to pension cutbacks (Bender, 2002; Fuchs, 1992). The MTA increased its fares from 50 to 60 cents and suspended capital improvement projects, while the city's university system (City University of New York [CUNY]) discontinued open enrollment and instituted tuition for the first time ever, the Department of Sanitation scaled down daily garbage pickups (except Sundays) and daily street rinsing in the summer, and public libraries reduced hours (Bloom & Lasner, 2016a; Detter & Fölster, 2017; Grogan & Proscio, 2000; Schill, Ellen, Schwartz, & Voicu, 2002).

In the entire city, sanitation workers went on several week-long strikes, laid-off police officers staged demonstrations, and residents even occupied a shuttered fire station, while trash on the streets piled up, crime increased, buildings burned and arsonists remained at large, and public health officials worried that the rotting garbage would cause disease outbreaks (Azzarone, 2022; Phillips-Fein, 2011). Some argue that the city systematically reduced its fire services, in particular in its poorest neighborhoods on the Lower East Side, in Harlem and Brooklyn, and the South Bronx (Flood, 2010). Indeed, New York City lost about 600,000 housing units due to accidental fires, arson, and abandonment from 1970 to 1980 (Flood, 2010). While these losses reflected a long-term trend, they were most likely exacerbated by the municipal fiscal crisis. About 30% of the fires were suspected to be arson (Soffer, 2010). In the Bronx, seven (out of 289) tracts lost more than 97% and 44 tracts lost more than 50% of their buildings to accidental fires, arson, and abandonment during the same time (Flood, 2010). Also, vacancies, tax delinquencies, and foreclosures increased (Zukin, 1989). The Bronx, central and northern Brooklyn, and Upper and Lower Manhattan were hit hardest by these public austerity measures, and some companies moving to the distant suburbs, contributing to the loss of affordable housing, severe neighborhood deterioration, the displacement of tens of thousands of residents leading to mass homelessness, and decreasing property values (Brower, 1989; Ferguson, 2007).

While local austerity measures disproportionately impacted lower- and middle-income residents, many of whom argued that the city systematically failed to address their needs, many corporations and financial institutions negotiated tax cuts and incentives, such as moving allowances or cut-rate electricity, and had tax incentives and grants that continued to fuel privatization trends, including massive new skyscraper office towers and hotels (Brash, 2011). Ironically, while some of these buildings were completed, some corporations started their urban exodus to the suburbs because of the city's worsening image (Greenberg, 2008). In sum, the austerity measures reduced New York City's liberal redistributive New Deal and managerialist approaches, which had focused on facilities, amenities, services, and benefit provision and maintenance for working- and middle-class New Yorkers, the public sector, including public infrastructure, and regulation. At the same time, the influence of organized labor and its allied social movements decreased (Rath et al., 2014). In this era, housing policy focused on affordable housing for working households (Kuttner, 2021; National Low Income Housing Coalition, 2020). While New York seemed to have started bouncing back as a whole, there was an increasing polarization of the labor and housing markets that was fueled by cuts to social programs, as evidenced in rapidly increasing housing prices and housing affordability challenges (Fitch, 1993).

New York's immediate post-bankruptcy period was punctuated by a 25-hour-long, citywide blackout in July 1977 that was caused by a heat wave and then a lightning storm in Westchester County that disabled two generators, overloading the remainder of the grid (Azzarone, 2022; Eng, 2022; Phillips-Fein, 2017). The outage affected nine million people and triggered accidental fires and arsons, vandalism, and looting by people who had lost their jobs, benefits, and hope. In addition, the Son of Sam murders by serial killer David Berkowitz occurred between December 1975 and July 1977 (Azzarone, 2022; Eng, 2022). All these fear-triggering events exacerbated public tension, slowing down investments and the city's recovery (Highsmith, 2015).

Buildings may have been burned by owners or third parties hired by them in order to collect insurance proceeds, or they may have been burned by residents or third parties to receive prime spots on waitlists for public housing (Dyja, 2021; Hassell, 1999). While the majority of fires were accidental, possibly triggered by neglect and overcrowding, others were clearly arson, particularly those occurring in already burned-out and abandoned buildings. These fires enabled scrappers to harvest valuable resources, including copper, wiring, and lead pipes (Flood, 2010).

New York City paid off its short-term debt in 1977/78 and was able to retire its federal obligations by 1983. These developments enabled the city to borrow again from select institutions, including banks holding its notes, pension funds, and state and federal governments (Sweeting & Dinneen, 2013). By the mid-1980s, the city's recovery was also aided by gradually decreasing crime, population gains, improving public schools and infrastructure, increasing MTA ridership, an increasing number of visitors and tourists, safer parks, and diminishing graffiti, all showing overall resilience, good risk tolerance, and a long tradition of entrepreneurship (Jackson, 2007a). Indeed, New York City celebrated Reggie Jackson's three home-run game to secure the New York Yankees World Series title over the Los Angeles Dodgers in the Bronx in October 1977. Enthusiasm generated by the Yankee championships in 1977 and again in 1978 were matched by the city's resurgent art world and the growing prominence of the SoHo and Tribeca (TRIangle BElow CAnal) galleries. Global art superstar Andy Warhol, who established the New York Academy of Art in Tribeca in 1980, reinforced the primacy of the city's art, fashion, and media scenes (Tippins, 2013).

Violent crime, especially among adolescents and young adults, increased again in the late 1980s and early 1990s, partly fueled by the prior heroin epidemic of the late 1960s and 1970s, then the wave of cocaine use facilitated by emerging street drug markets of the late 1970s and 1980s, and finally the crack epidemic and the rapid expansion of drug retailing in many inner cities in the early 1990s, culminating in the *New York Post* headline "Dave, Do Something." This headline caused Mayor David Dinkins to establish the Safe Streets/Safe City program and hire 5,000 additional police officers just before he left office (Manshel, 2020, p. 1). In 1994, Mayor Rudolph Giuliani (1994–2001), who won the election partly based on an increased fear of crime, and the New York City Police Department (NYPD) launched a citywide quality-of-life policing campaign based on James Wilson and George Kelling's 1982 broken windows hypothesis to re-attract businesses and residents (Dyja, 2021). The hypothesis worked on the assumption that sustained targeting of minor offenses prevents more serious crimes, facilitated by CompStat, a software introduced in 1994 to map crimes in real time and enabling top-level police officers to hold precinct commanders accountable (Fagan & MacDonald, 2013). The goal of this quality-of-life campaign was to instantly take a (minor) offender into custody, holding them until they appeared in court a day or two later (Vitale, 2008). This practice replaced the previous custom, where officers issued summons on the spot and ordered offenders to appear in court at a future date, although most offenders did not show up, hoping not to be tracked by the slow and overburdened judicial system (Vitale, 2008).

Examples of minor offenses are fare beating by jumping MTA's turnstiles, jaywalking, littering, graffiti, sleeping and urinating in public, earning money by washing windshields of cars waiting at traffic lights by the so-called squeegee people, and public consumption of alcohol or other illegal substances (Onishi, 1994). The incidence of some minor offenses had gradually increased partly due to the reduction of mental health-care services and deinstitutionalization since the 1960s as well as the introduction of local austerity measures right after New York City's fiscal crisis in 1975 (Botein & Hetling, 2016).

As part of its quality-of-life campaign, the city designated Pennsylvania Station as an area where the homeless could sleep on the (cold and barren) floor (Dordick, 1997). The NYPD's tactics were zero tolerance, stop and frisk, civil enforcement, flexible deployment, and establishing new rules and regulations (Vitale, 2008). Zero tolerance assigns officers to hotspots where they aggressively enforce the law (Vitale, 2008). Stop and frisk, widely condemned as excessive, authorized officers to stop people for any reason to search for illegal drugs and weapons (Vitale, 2008). Civil enforcement aims to develop cooperative relationships between the NYPD and other city departments and agencies, in particular the New York City Law Department, to enforce rules and regulations for minor offenses (Vitale, 2008). Flexible deployment is practiced by those officers not assigned to 911 duty who proactively address anticipated crimes based on neighborhood intelligence or CompStat, such as by saturating a hotspot (Vitale, 2008).

FURTHER INFORMATION

Flood, J. (2010). *The fires: How a computer formula, big ideas, and the best of intentions burned down New York City—and determined the future of cities*. Penguin.

Freeman, J. B. (2000). *Working class New York: Life and labor since World War II*. The New Press.

Holtzman, B. (2021). *The long crisis: New York City and the path to neoliberalism*. Oxford University Press.

Phillips-Fein, K. (2017). *Fear city: New York's fiscal crisis and the rise of austerity politics*. Picador.

HOUSING

HOUSING SUPPLY IN NEW YORK CITY

Over the past few decades, many major cities in the U.S., especially on the east and west coasts, have had high population and economic growth and thus share many land use and housing challenges, including scarce land, relatively tight land use regulations, and an imbalance between limited housing supply and near unlimited housing demand (Anacker, 2024). This imbalance has led to housing shortages, contributing to severe housing affordability challenges for most of their residents (Anacker, 2024). New York City, with its population of 8.3 million as of July 2023, has long been the most populous and dense city in the United States, increasing from about 7.1 million in 1980, when its decade-long population loss had reached a trough, to 7.3 million in 1990, 8 million in 2000, about 8.2 million in 2010, and 8.8 million in 2020, then decreasing to about 8.3 million in 2023 after the COVID-19 pandemic (Caldwell, 2005; Capperis, de la Roca, Ellen, Karfunkel, Kuai, Moriarty, Steil, Stern, Suher, Weselcouch, Willis, & Yager, 2014; Office of the New York State Comptroller, 2023). Similar to the increase in population, there has been an increase in the number of households in New York City, from about 3.11 million in 2010 to 3.37 million in 2020 (City of New York, n.d.f). However, over time New York City's household size has decreased from 2.57 in 2010 to 2.55 in 2020 (City of New York, n.d.f).

In terms of population density (i.e., the number of people per square mile), there were over 29,000 people per square mile in

DOI: 10.1201/9781003624172-6

New York City in 2020, while there were 402.7, 411.2, and 428.7 people per square mile in the State of New York in 2000, 2010, and 2020, respectively, and 79.7, 87.4, and 93.8 people per square mile in the United States in 2000, 2010, and 2020, respectively (City of New York, n.d.b; U.S. Bureau of the Census, n.d.a). In 2010, New York City's densest neighborhoods were Manhattan's Upper East Side (109,000 people per square mile), Stuyvesant Town/Turtle Bay (92,000), Lower East Side/Chinatown (95,000), and Central Harlem (82,000) and the Bronx's Kingsbridge Heights/Moshulu (79,000), the most recent numbers available as of this writing (Capperis et al., 2014).

Over time, New York City's housing unit density (i.e., the number of housing units per square mile) has increased from about 9,700 in 1980; to 9,900 in 1990; 10,600 in 2000; and 11,100 in 2010, the most recent numbers available as of this writing (Capperis et al., 2014). There were 163, 172, and 180 housing units per square mile in the State of New York in 2000, 2010, and 2020, respectively, compared to 33, 35, and 40 housing units per square mile in the United States in 2000, 2010, and 2020, respectively (U.S. Bureau of the Census, n.d.a).

Over the past few decades, New York City has had a limited, regulated, and moderately increasing housing supply. More specifically, there has been an overall increase in housing units, increasing from 2.941 million housing units in 1980, to 2.992 million units in 1990, to 3.200 million units in 2000, to 3.371 million units in 2010, to 3.618 million units in 2020, and to 3,705,000 units in 2023, the largest stock in the city's history (Bloom & Lasner, 2016e; New York City Rent Guidelines Board, 2024; U.S. Bureau of the Census, n.d.a). In sum, the number of housing units in New York City has grown slowly but steadily over the past decades. However, the overall increase in the number of housing units has not positively impacted New York City's persistent housing affordability crisis.

Over the past three decades, New York City has had a decrease in the number of low-cost (i.e., rents of less than $1,500 per month) and an increase in the number of high-cost (i.e., rents of more than $2,300 per month) rental housing units, based on inflation-adjusted rents. More specifically, New York City had a net loss of more than 600,000 units with rents of $1,500 or less, while it had a net increase of almost 75,000 units with rents of $5,000 or more (City of New York, n.d.a). Reasons for the decrease in the number of units with relatively low rents include rent increases, the construction of new units at any rent level, alterations and conversions, changes in unit availability, and tenure conversions (City of New York, n.d.a).

On the one hand, New York City's limited housing supply has been influenced by natural, economic, political, and location- and building-specific factors. On the other hand, its near-unlimited, unregulated, and vastly increasing housing demand has been influenced by demographic and socioeconomic factors. In terms of the natural factors that have influenced housing supply, New York City is a city of two islands (Manhattan and Staten Island) created by glaciers during the last ice age more than 12,000 years ago; thus, many areas are constrained due to the presence of rivers, straits, and bays, such as the Hudson River, the East River, and the Jamaica Bay, all of which translates into a naturally limited land supply (Glaeser & Gyourko, 2018; Melosi, 2020).

Also, Manhattan has some geological and pedological (i.e., soil) constraints. On the one hand, there is dark gray surface bedrock, called Manhattan schist, as well as Inwood marble and Fordham gneiss, all of which are extremely durable, providing a solid anchorage and great support for skyscrapers downtown near Manhattan's southern tip, the original location of Dutch settlement and the current center of finance in the country, and Midtown, the largest business district in the nation, containing the Empire State and Chrysler Buildings, Park Avenue, and Times Square (Anderson, 2015; Azzarone, 2022; Bender, 2002; Blake, 2020; d'Almeida, 2018; Koeppel, 2015; Melosi, 2020). On the other hand, there are areas filled with glacial till with low bearing capacity that can only support low- and mid-rise buildings, such as in Greenwich Village, SoHo, or (Manhattan's) Chinatown (McPhee, 1983). Yet others still counter that bedrock is not necessarily needed to build skyscrapers, as evidenced in many major cities, including Chicago (Glaeser & Cutler, 2021).

Interestingly, Barr (2016) states that the skyscrapers' "battle for place" was not only determined by geology or pedology but also by demographic, socioeconomic, and housing market factors. To explain the current absence of skyscrapers between downtown and

Midtown, he points out that after the 1830s, middle- and upper-income residents who lived and worked downtown, typically merchants, moved north to neighborhoods such as Washington Square Park, Gramercy Park, St. Mark's Place, and southern Fifth Avenue, bypassing and thus avoiding low-rise, low-income neighborhoods such as (Manhattan's) Chinatown, Greenwich Village, and the Lower East Side, described by Jacob Riis in 1890 (Barr, 2016; Bender, 2002).

While the middle- and upper-income residents moved north, their workplaces were still at the southern tip of Manhattan, requiring them to commute between homes and workplaces. This split was facilitated by the horse-drawn omnibus, introduced in 1829, the horse-drawn streetcar, introduced in 1832 and embedded in rails, the steam-powered locomotion streetcar, introduced in 1837, and then steam-powered elevated railroads, introduced in 1868, all of which enabled mass transportation (Nevlus, 2018; Osman, 2011). Barr (2016) argues that the historic lock-in process in (Manhattan's) Chinatown, Greenwich Village, and the Lower East Side has remained, leading to a current lack of demand for skyscrapers north of Chambers and south of 14th Street.

In terms of the economic and political factors that have influenced housing supply, New York City has had relatively high construction costs due to relatively high local unionized wages in the construction sector, partly due to the high cost of living; the relatively high unionization rate compared to other U.S. cities; the relatively high costs of building materials, including concrete; high energy costs; the permanent traffic congestion, which makes transporting materials to sites expensive; and relatively high fees (Brenzel, 2017; Freeman, 2000; Gurock, 2019).

New York State has relatively high property tax rates compared to other states, in addition to high state and municipal income taxes (Cammenga, 2020). As land and house prices are very high, homeowners face high tax bills (Glaeser, 2011). Interestingly, New York State has higher property tax rates for multifamily rental, condominium, and cooperative developments than for single-family homes (Schill & Scafidi, 1999). Thus, developers and builders negotiate individual tax abatements which may be controversial in some cases (Phillips-Fein, 2017; Salins, 1999).

Some argue that New York City's regulations are relatively stringent due to restrictions in land use, zoning, building code and fire safety, including provisions for accessibility and seismic activity, air rights, landmark status, mandatory environmental impact assessments, parking or open space requirements, and the Uniform Land Use Review Process (ULURP), passed in 1975 and effective since 1977 (Fahim, 2010). Amended in 1989 through New York City's Charter Revision, ULURP gives Community Boards (CBs) and residents the opportunity to review proposals and make suggestions about land use decisions, such as zoning changes, urban renewal plans, acquisition and disposition of municipal properties, and special permits (Berg, 2018; Fainstein, 2001). Then, the suggestions of this transparent and democratic but possibly politically contentious process are passed on to the appropriate borough president's office, the City Planning Commission (CPC), and then City Council (Berg, 2018; Melosi, 2020; Plotch, 2020). These regulations may have influenced housing supply, contributing to smaller or delayed supply, higher house prices, greater volatility of house prices, and less volatility of new housing construction, possibly leading to an implicit tax (Kantor et al., 2012).

New York City's limited housing supply has also been influenced by location- and building-specific factors, including access to parks, the public transportation system, and cultural attractions. After the implementation of austerity measures in the 1970s, funding for parks decreased, contributing to deferred maintenance and neglect, with some parks becoming derelict spaces with degraded ecosystems and crime (Birge-Liberman, 2017). While 30,000 to 60,000 temporary employees, primarily funded by federal programs during the Great Depression, took care of New York City's park system in 1934, fewer than 5,000 employees did so in 1988 (Soffer, 2010). Comparing annual operating subsidies per agency for FY 2018, New York City spent $380 million for parks, $373 million for libraries, and $188 million for cultural affairs, the most recent numbers available as of this writing (Regional Plan Association, 2018). However, park investments have been distributed unevenly. Thus, the New York City Department of Parks and Recreation established the equity-based Community Parks Initiative in 2014, prioritizing investment in neighborhood parks with the greatest need (American Planning Association, 2020; City of New York, n.d.i). Currently, New York City has about 1,900 public parks, including the better-known Brooklyn Bridge Park, Bryant Park in Midtown Manhattan, the Harlem Promenade, Prospect Park in Brooklyn, and Tompkins Square Park near Stuyvesant Town in Manhattan, as well as many others only known to their surrounding neighborhood residents (Loughran, 2017; Mensch, 2018).

Lastly, building-specific factors that have influenced housing supply include New York City's many amenities, with cultural attractions such as Carnegie Hall, the Museum of Modern Art (MoMa), and Broadway, and recreational attractions like Central Park and the High Line, all in Manhattan (Glaeser, Gyourko, & Saks, 2003). The 843-acre Central Park, which was first suggested in 1857 and designed by Frederick Law Olmsted and Calvert Vaux, followed the modern English tradition of landscape architecture. Part of the park is built on the former site of Seneca Village, already discussed in Chapter 3 (Central Park Conservancy, n.d.).

Over recent decades, the High Line, which can be characterized as an "idealized urban wasteland" or an "idealized rural idyll," has been one of the city's most popular attractions and probably the second most well-known park after Central Park (Baker, 2017, p. 114; Lindner, 2017). In 1999, Joshua David, a freelance writer, and Robert Hammond, an entrepreneur, established the grassroots, nonprofit group Friends of the High Line (FHL) to convert a derelict, elevated freight steel railway snaking through the West Side of Manhattan, running from the Meatpacking District to the Hudson Yards, to a "rails-to-trails" elevated park development. The High Line is an about 1.5-mile or 21-block-long, elevated, linear, public park, greenway, and trail that can be accessed with 10 staircase entries. Designed by James Corner Field Operations with Diller, Scofidio + Renfro and Piet Oudolf, it opened in three phases in 2009, 2012, and 2014 (Lindner & Rosa, 2017; Rosa & Lindner, 2017).

HOUSING DEMAND IN NEW YORK CITY

Although there has been an overall increase in the number of housing units, there has been a decrease in the proportion of housing units that are affordable in recent years and decades. While

New York City experienced a suburban and exurban exodus in March, April, and May 2020, housing demand gradually increased, especially in late 2022, when thousands of migrants and asylum seekers arrived in the city (Anacker, 2022; Ferré-Sadurní, 2024).

Housing demand is influenced by demographic and socioeconomic factors. In terms of demographic factors, hundreds of thousands of migrants and immigrants have moved to New York City to pursue opportunities, such as working, studying, or starting a business (City of New York, 2014; Wilkerson, 2010). Migration waves occurred in the first half of the 20th century, when thousands of Black/African American migrants from the South moved to inner cities in the North during the Great Migration and when thousands of GIs returned from World War II and started a national baby boom in the late 1940s (Melosi, 2020). Immigration waves occurred from the 1850s to the early 1920s and from the 1970s on, when millions of immigrants came to the United States (Glaeser, 2005).

Housing demand has also been influenced by socioeconomic factors, in particular household incomes and household wealth. Typically, there are differences in household incomes between renters versus owners. In the case of New York City, renters had a median household income of $70,000 compared to owners, who had a median household income of $122,000 in 2023 (City of New York, n.d.a). More specifically, 24% of all renters (about 574,400) earned less than $25,000 annually in 2023, compared to 13% of all owners (about 148,400; City of New York, n.d.a). Thirty-six percent of renters (about 835,600) earned more than $100,000, compared to 59% of owners (about 650,100) did so (City of New York, n.d.a). Indeed, the inflation-adjusted median household income of renters increased from $50,000 to $70,000, it increased from $98,000 to $122,000 for owners from 2021 to 2023 (City of New York, n.d.a). Nevertheless, income increases may be lower than housing cost increases, still resulting in housing affordability challenges.

Household wealth is difficult to analyze due to the reluctance of many high-net-worth individuals (HNWIs) to answer household surveys. However, there is anecdotal evidence that a relatively high number of HNWIs has been outbidding those with fewer resources over the past few decades, thus partly causing house prices and rents in New York City to increase (Atkinson, Burrows, Glucksberg, Ho, Knowles, & Rhodes, 2017; Frank, 1999; 2007; Glantz, 2019; Harrington, 2016; Stiman, 2024; Venkatesh, 2013).

HOUSING AFFORDABILITY CHALLENGES IN NEW YORK CITY

In contrast to New York City's housing supply, which has been limited, regulated, and has only moderately increased, its housing demand has been near-unlimited, unregulated, and has rapidly increased over time, contributing to an imbalance between housing supply and housing demand. This long-term imbalance may have contributed to increasing land and house prices as well as rents, also contributing to New York City's perpetual and persistent housing affordability crisis, which has been going on for almost 100 years (Schwartz, 2019). For example, from 2002 to 2017, median gross rents increased by over 37%, while median renter incomes only increased by 20% (City of New York, n.d.h). In sum, New York City has been one of the least affordable major cities in the U.S. for decades (Gross & Savitch, 2023).

New York City has a relatively high rentership rate that has been almost twice as high as its homeownership rate over the past few decades (Capperis et al., 2014). The rentership rate gradually but slightly decreased from 77% in 1980 to 66% in 2009, but it has slightly increased since then to 69% in 2024 (Capperis et al., 2014; City of New York, n.d.a; Lander, 2024; New York City Rent Guidelines Board, 2024). New Yorkers disproportionately live in market-rate housing (48% of the entire rental housing stock or about 1.1 million units), followed by rent-stabilized housing (42%, about 960,000 units), public housing (7%, about 168,000 units), other regulated housing (2%, about 52,000 units), and rent-controlled housing (1%, about 24,000 units; New York City Rent Guidelines Board, 2024). In the near and distant future, New York City's rentership rate is expected to increase, as new developments will be overwhelmingly medium- to high-density multifamily housing and because homeownership has become unaffordable for many, partly due to the high mortgage interest rates, which started to increase in the spring of 2022 (Anacker, 2024; Ellen & Karfunkel, 2016).

An indicator of a housing affordability challenge is the proportion of renters who face a relatively high housing cost burden. As mentioned above, whereas housing cost-burdened residents pay more than 30% of their (gross) household incomes for housing, severely housing cost-burdened residents pay more than 50% (Anacker & Li, 2016; City of New York, 2017a). In 2023, 18% of renter households were rent burdened and 25% were severely rent burdened (City of New York, n.d.a). While the housing cost burden gradually increased between 1965 and 2021, it decreased in 2023 for the first time in decades due to very recent average household income increases after the COVID-19 pandemic, possibly indicating workers gaining or having voice in retentions or hires, household members entering the workforce (again), and more higher-income households moving to than leaving New York City (New York City Rent Guidelines Board, 2024). A high housing cost burden may translate into missing or alternate rental payments that impact a household's budget, leaving less to pay for food, utilities, transportation to work, and health and childcare expenditures, as well as reducing savings for emergencies, retirement, and other opportunities, such as pursuing higher education or starting a small business (Anacker, 2019; City of New York, n.d.a; Colburn & Walter, 2025). A high housing cost burden may also translate into crowded or severely crowded housing units and low vacancy rates (Helmreich, 2013). While crowded units have more than one person per room, severely crowded units have more than 1.5 (City of New York, 2017a).

Most of New York City's homeowners have faced high land and house prices, leading to a relatively high housing cost burden and mortgage and property tax affordability challenges and a relatively low overall homeownership rate but relatively high cooperative and condominium ownership rates (Helmreich, 2013). Many New Yorkers purchase cooperative housing units (28% of the entire owner-occupied housing stock) and condominiums (11%), which may be more affordable than 2–3 family and single-family units that may be less affordable (61%; New York City Rent Guidelines Board, 2024; Willis, Austensen, Moriarty, Rosoff, & Sanders, 2016).

Some may argue that New York City's high proportion of housing cost-burdened residents may translate into its relatively high proportion of (severely) crowded housing units (City of New York, n.d.a). In the 19th and 20th centuries, many scholars discussed poor physical housing conditions, including insufficient amounts of light and air, poor hygiene, crowding, and household poverty, and focused on common communicable diseases (Bowdler, Quercia, & Smith, 2010). Common diseases included smallpox, typhoid, malaria, yellow fever, tuberculosis, cholera, and diphtheria, among many others (Dolkart, 2016). This discussion was revisited during the somewhat recent COVID-19 pandemic, especially in terms of the relationship between crowding and the spread of COVID-19 (Ali, Connolly, & Keil, 2023; Anacker, 2022; Seidlein, Alabaster, Deen, & Knudsen, 2021). In the 21st century, many scholars who discuss crowding and household poverty focus on stressful situations within households, as reported during the Great Recession, when foreclosed borrowers moved in with relatives or friends (Center on Budget and Policy Priorities, 2019; Kingsley, Smith, & Price, 2009).

In 2023, 8% of all householders in New York City lived in a crowded unit, and 9.2% of all renters did (City of New York, n.d.a; New York City Rent Guidelines Board, 2024). However, there were differences by race, ethnicity, nativity, and the age of householders (City of New York, n.d.a). About 4% of non-Hispanic White New Yorkers lived in a crowded unit, compared to 7% of Black/African American, 11% of Hispanic, and 10% of Asian New Yorkers (City of New York, n.d.a). About 12% of foreign-born and about 5% of elderly householders lived in a crowded unit (City of New York, n.d.a). The argument about the correlation between crowding and rent burden, which is different than causation, may work well in the case of non-Hispanic Whites, who have a relatively low rate of crowding (4%) and a moderate rate of severely rent burdened households (22%; City of New York, n.d.a). However, it may work less well in the case of Blacks/African Americans, who also have a somewhat low rate of crowding (7%) but a high rate of severely rent-burdened households (28%; City of New York, n.d.a).

New York City has had relatively low vacancy rates, indicating an undersupply of housing (Schwartz, 2019). In 2023, with the lowest rate since the inception of the New York City Housing and Vacancy Survey (NYCHVS) in 1965, 1.41% of all rental units were vacant, down from 4.54% in 2021, 1.8% in 2015, and 3.6% in 2010 (City of New York, n.d.a; New York City Rent Guidelines Board, 2024; Schwartz, 2019). These proportions are below the 5% threshold that defines a state housing emergency, which is also below a rate considered healthy by state legislators and housing providers, and it permits rent regulation to be active under State law (City of New York, n.d.a, 2010; Collins & Staff of the New York City Rent Guidelines Board, 2020; New York City Rent Guidelines Board, 2024). New York City's vacancy rate was last above 5% in the late 1920s (Fogelson, 2013).

However, vacancy rates differed among types of rental housing: the vacancy rate of rent-stabilized housing was 0.98% and the rate of public housing was 1.21% in 2023 (City of New York, n.d.a). Vacancy rates also differed among units with different monthly asking rents: units with rents of less than $1,650 had a vacancy rate of 0.65%, while units with rents of more than $1,650 had a vacancy rate of 2.16% (City of New York, n.d.a). Interestingly, vacant units were unavailable for several different reasons in 2023. Of those units unavailable for two or more reasons (36%), 26% were held for seasonal, recreational, occasional use, 18% were awaiting or undergoing renovation, 6% were held as vacant, and 4% were in a legal dispute in 2023 (City of New York, n.d.a).

In sum, the imbalance between housing supply and housing demand may have contributed to different outcomes for renters than homeowners. Most of New York City's renters have faced high rents, leading to a relatively high housing cost burden and housing affordability challenges, (severely) crowded housing units, and low vacancy rates, ultimately contributing to a relatively high rentership rate (Helmreich, 2013). Most of New York City's homeowners have faced high land and house prices, leading to a relatively high housing cost burden and mortgage and property tax affordability challenges and a relatively low overall homeownership rate but relatively high condominium and cooperative ownership rate (Helmreich, 2013). New Yorkers disproportionately purchase condominiums and cooperative housing units, which may be more affordable to some compared with 2–3 family and single-family units that may be less affordable (Willis et al., 2016). For example, the homeownership rate for condominiums was 40% and 69% for cooperatives in 2023, with the remainder being renter-occupied (City of New York, n.d.a).

HOUSING ACTIVISM IN NEW YORK CITY

New York City's housing activism, including its self-help housing movement, has had a long history since the mid-20th century, driven by its many community activists and community development corporations (CDCs; Marwell, 2007; Saegert & Winkel, 1998; Wolf-Powers, 2014). In the 1950s and 1960s, most cities in the U.S. experienced so-called White flight to the suburbs, facilitated by many federal policies passed in the 1930s, including the Federal Home Loan Bank Act in 1932, the Home Owners' Loan Corporation (HOLC) in 1933, the Federal Deposit Insurance Corporation (FDIC) in 1933, the National Housing Act in 1934, and Fannie Mae in 1938 (Anacker, 2024). White flight to the suburbs was also facilitated by the Federal Aid Highway Act of 1956 (Clergé, 2019; von Hoffman, 2003). It was sometimes triggered by abandonment, arson, and violence, resulting in a decrease in the number of habitable, affordable housing units in the 1960s and 1970s (Capperis et al., 2014).

In the 1970s, New York City's property tax delinquency and vacancy rates were at record highs, while tax collections were at a record low (Brower, 1989). Thus, in 1974, community activists founded the Urban Homesteading Assistance Board (UHAB), a citywide organization that provided technical and financial support to the many self-help cooperatives and homesteaders in the city (City of New York, 2021; Hassell, 1999; Zelasnic, 2007). In addition, New York City Council passed Local Law 45 in 1976, allowing the City to rapidly pursue tax-delinquent (*in rem*) foreclosures of buildings after one year of tax delinquency (Citizens Housing and Planning Council, 1995; Stern & Yager, 2016). After the City bought and then sold these buildings at foreclosure auctions, they realized that the new owners often fell into tax arrears quite quickly (Holtzman, 2021). Thus, they began to buy and operate them (Jaffe, 2007). At its peak in 1986, New York City owned and managed 40,000 units in occupied housing and 55,000 units in vacant buildings (New York City Rent Guidelines Board, 2024).

Also in the 1970s, community housing activists urged Mayor Ed Koch to transfer *in rem* units to new owners through several programs administered by the Division of Alternative Management Program (DAMP), a (progressive) division established within the Department of Housing Preservation and Development (HPD) in 1979 (New York City Rent Guidelines Board, 2024; NYU Furman Center, n.d.). DAMP administrators select alternative managers of previously tax-delinquent *in rem* buildings now owned by Housing Development Fund Companies (HDFCs), which are typically nonprofit organizations (City of New York, 2021; NYU Furman Center, n.d.). Another example of DAMP's programs is the Tenant Interim Lease Program (TIL, active since 1978), which focuses on rehabilitating city-owned, vacant, multifamily properties and building new, small homes on free and vacant land where limited-equity, tenant-owned cooperatives pursue urban homesteading (City of New York, n.d.c; n.d.d; Holtzman, 2016; NYU Furman Center, n.d.)

RECENT MAYORAL HOUSING PLANS IN NEW YORK CITY

To address housing affordability issues, many New York City mayors have created long-term housing plans in the past few decades. Examples of recent mayoral housing plans are Mayor Ed Koch's 1985 *Ten-year Housing Plan*, Mayor Michael Bloomberg's 2002 *Bloomberg Plan*, the 2003 *New Housing Marketplace Plan* (NHMP), and *PlanNYC 2030* in 2007. Also, there is Mayor Bill de Blasio's *Housing New York: A Five-Borough Ten-year Housing Plan*, unveiled in May 2014, followed by *Housing New York 2.0* in November 2017 and *YOUR Home NYC* in January 2020 (City of New York, 2014; 2017b; 2020; New York City Housing Preservation and Development, n.d.).

After launching the *Ten-year Housing Plan* in 1985, Koch extended it to 12 years in 1988 and expanded the initial goal of rehabilitating and building 100,000 mixed-income housing units to 252,000 units over 10 years in 1989, about 8% of the city's total housing stock (Schill et al., 2002; Soffer, 2016). Of the 252,000 units, 84,000 units (33%) were to be newly constructed and 168,000 (66%) to be rehabilitated (Brower, 1989). This Plan became one of the most enduring achievements of Koch's mayoralty (Schill et al., 2002; Soffer, 2010).

Koch initially committed $4.2 billion, the largest municipal investment in housing in U.S. history, to the *Ten-year Housing Plan* (Soffer, 2016). He eventually expanded funding to $5.1 billion, financed and cross-subsidized through several local public institutions, including the New York City Housing Development Corporation (NYCHDC), New York City's Municipal Water Finance Authority, and the Port Authority of New York and New Jersey (PANYNJ; City of New York, 2010; New York City Housing Development Corporation, n.d.a; n.d.b). Funding also came from the private sector, New York State, and the federal government (Van Ryzin & Genn, 1999). On a per capita basis, Koch's *Ten-year Housing Plan* allocated about $102 per resident for housing, compared to an average of $5.90 in other large cities (Berenyi, 1989). Koch implemented this Plan, followed by his two successors (Bloom & Lasner, 2016e; City of New York, 2014; Powell, 2009; Terry, 1990).

Mayor Michael Bloomberg launched the *Bloomberg Plan*, which had the goal of producing 60,000 affordable housing units by 2006, then 68,000 units by 2008 (Angotti, 2014). In 2003, Bloomberg launched the NHMP with an initial goal of constructing or preserving 65,000 below-market rental housing units affordable to low- and medium-income families by 2008, adjusted to 165,000 units in 2010, and actually realized by 2014 (City of New York, 2010; Mogilevich, 2016).

Mayor Bill de Blasio's *Housing New York: A Five-borough, Ten Year Plan* was one of the most ambitious housing plans in the country, with its goal of building 80,000 and preserving 120,000 affordable, high-quality housing units (200,000 units total) by 2024 (City of New York, 2014; 2017b; 2019; New York City Housing Preservation and Development, n.d.). In 2017, about 20% of all new housing units built were part of the Plan (City of New York, n.d.h). The de Blasio administration estimated that the Plan would cost about $41.4 billion, with $30 billion (73%) from the private and $11.4 billion (27%) from the public sector (Busà, 2017).

Housing New York 2.0 changed the date of the initial goal of building 80,000 and preserving 120,000 affordable housing units proposed in the previous Plan from 2024 to 2022 and added a new goal of building an additional 100,000 affordable units by 2026 (City of New York, 2017b; New York City Housing Preservation and Development, n.d.). The updated plan had the goal of creating and preserving more homes for residents with household incomes ranging from extremely low to moderate, seniors, and people with disabilities, among others (City of New York, 2013, 2017b).

In sum, some of New York City's mayoral housing plans have been the largest local place-based programs in the history of the United States. While they have addressed affordable housing shortages, they have only put a dent—albeit a massive one—into addressing New York City's affordable housing crisis.

FURTHER INFORMATION

Lander, B. (2024, January 17). *Spotlight: New York City's rental housing market*. https://comptroller.nyc.gov/reports/spotlight-new-york-citys-rental-housing-market/

New York City Rent Guidelines Board. (2024). *Housing NYC: Rents, markets, and trends 2024*. https://rentguidelinesboard.cityofnewyork.us/wp-content/uploads/2024/10/2024-HNYC-Book.pdf

Office of the New York State Comptroller. (2023). *NYC's shifting population: The latest statistics*. https://www.osc.ny.gov/files/reports/osdc/pdf/report-15-2024.pdf?utm_medium=email&utm_source=govdelivery

Plunz, R. (2016). *A history of housing in New York City*. Columbia University Press.

GOVERNMENT AND GOVERNANCE

Local governments (i.e., counties, cities, and special districts) provide many public services through their police, fire, medical emergency, water, sewer, and roads departments, as well as public transportation, housing, and parks and recreation services, funded by the federal and state governments, as well as property and income taxes, service fees, and other revenues (Gross & Savitch, 2023). New York City's government consists of the following elected people: the mayor, the New York City Council (with 51 council members), the Borough Presidents (including the five borough boards and 59 community boards (CBs)), the district attorneys, the Independent Budget Office (IBO), the public advocate, and the comptroller (Fainstein, 2001).

New York City's publicly elected mayor, the most powerful head in the municipal political system, signs and then administers laws, prepares and presents the municipality's budget for Council approval, and serves as the chief executive, controlling the municipality's government by heading municipal services and thus implementing policy, among many other tasks, as laid out in the City Charter (Berg, 2018). Over the past several decades, New York City has had a strong-mayor model with powerful political and administrative leadership, making this person the focal point of the municipal political system (Berg, 2018).

The mayor appoints the First Deputy Mayor as well as deputy mayors to head offices with specific executive competencies. Examples of these deputy mayors are the Deputy Mayor for

Strategic Initiatives, the Deputy Mayor for Housing, Economic Development, and Workforce, the Deputy Mayor for Health and Human Services, the Chief Technology Officer, and the Office of Efficiency.

The New York City Council is the legislative body of the city and is thus responsible for passing bills, which become laws and may be vetoed by the mayor, although a mayoral veto may be overturned by the Council (Berg, 2018). The Council is a powerful decision maker, as it has sole approval authority over the city's budget, which is prepared and presented by the mayor (Berg, 2018). The Council also has the power to approve or reject zoning changes, city or community development plans, and special purpose zoning (overlay) districts (Busà, 2017). The 51 publicly elected members of the different council districts select the Council's president or speaker, who, along with the mayor and the Deputy Mayor of Housing and Economic Development, has one of the most powerful governmental posts in New York City (David & Hammond, 2011).

New York City's City Planning Commission (CPC), whose chair is also the head of the Department of City Planning (DCP), adopts or vetoes recommendations of the DCP and then passes the amendments to the zoning text or zoning map on to the City Council, which votes the amendments into law (Moss, 2017). The commission consists of 13 members: the mayor appoints the chair and six members, each borough present appoints one member, and the publicly elected Public Advocate appoints one member; the Public Advocate was the former City Council President before the Charter Revision in 1989 and has served as public ombudsperson or watchdog, addressing concerns of citizens and facilitating information transfer from agencies to the public, since 1993 (Berg, 2018).

Local governments have many kinds of relationships with state governments. State governments grant local governments powers and rights ("home rule") based on Dillon's Rule (1872; Gross & Savitch, 2023). For example, they allow local governments to select governmental institutions and procedures, such as drawing their own municipal charters, as well as to deliver public services, as mentioned above (Berg, 2018). In addition, state governments fund many local policies and programs, including in education, health and human services, economic development, and housing (Berg, 2018). Furthermore, in the case of New York State the

State Comptroller, state governments monitor local public finances (Berg, 2018). Moreover, state governments may control local governments' ability to raise some revenues beyond property taxes and some components of sales taxes, such as through congestion pricing (Berg, 2018). Congestion pricing started on January 5, 2025 and, intending to relieve traffic congestion and air pollution, applies to most vehicular traffic in Manhattan's Central Business District south of 61st Street from 5 am to 9 am on weekdays and from 9 am to 9 pm on weekends (Fields, 2025). Revenues of congestion pricing will be invested in public transportation (Schwab, 2025). During the first few months of 2025, traffic decreased and revenues increased, although the political fate of congestion pricing is uncertain as of this writing (Fields, 2025).

Some argue that New York City's mayor, with its more than two dozen departments, New York City Council, borough presidents, community boards, district attorneys, the Independent Budget Office, public advocates, and the comptroller preserve expertise and competency. Others argue that New York City's government system is fragmented (i.e., not unified or coordinated), governance is overly complex, and there are hundreds of formal and informal private and nonprofit entities, institutions, and actors, many of which are competing against or collaborating with each other (Gross & Savitch, 2023; Hyra, 2008). Nevertheless, New York City's government and governance are quite effective, resulting in a highly productive city (Gross & Savitch, 2023).

An example of two state governments effectively collaborating in the New York Metropolitan Statistical Area (MSA) is the Port Authority of New York and New Jersey (PANYNJ), a joint venture between New York and New Jersey. In 1921, after many years of competition among airports, marine terminals, bridges, tunnels, and bus terminals and programs in New York State and New Jersey, U.S. Congress allowed the two states to establish the Port of New York Authority, the first large bi-state authority in the U.S., which was later renamed PANYNJ (Doig, Erie, & Mackenzie, 2013). The Authority was charged with unifying the system and moving freight and people more efficiently in a district that ranged from Long Island to eastern and central New Jersey and from Sandy Hook in New York Harbor up the Hudson River to Westchester (Steinberg, 2014).

The Authority followed many of the recommendations from the Regional Plan of New York and Its Environs (1929), based on the Plan of Chicago ("Burnham Plan", 1909), advocating for regional collaboration and projecting the region's population to be 20 million by 1965 with an expanded central business district, envisioning slum clearance and urban renewal without manufacturing facilities downtown, and advocating for a balanced transportation approach with mass rapid transit facilities, three circumferential highways, and five river crossings (Bender, 2002; Caro, 1974; Johnson, 1996).

While the Regional Plan was the world's first long-range metropolitan plan, it was nevertheless not an official document, having been created by the nonprofit Regional Plan Association (RPA), which was headed by banking and business executives and funded by major foundations and financial, insurance, and real estate corporations, such as the Russell Sage Foundation, the Rockefeller Foundation, the Carnegie Foundation, First National Bank, Morgan Stanley, Equitable Trust, the New York Central, Penn Central, and Jersey Central Railroads, and other railroads (Bender, 2002; Kantor, 1994; Regional Plan Association, n.d.). While the members of the RPA did not have the power to implement the Regional Plan, they nevertheless had great influence over the governor of New York State and the mayor of New York City, as well as developers in the region (Johnson, 1996; Mele 2000). The foundations, corporations, and families in the RPA may have benefitted from these land-use changes through increased land and property values, as well as increased rents (Flood, 2010). In 1968, the RPA published the Second Regional Plan, funded by the Rockefeller and Ford Foundations, focused on reversing urban decline and spurring downtown growth, while also discussing technology and automobile orientation and designating regional subcenters for offices (Bender, 2002; Manshel, 2020). The Third Regional Plan, released in 1996, continued RPA's regional-comprehensive approach and dealt with regional growth, although it focused on ecology, balancing the economy, equity, and the environment; the Fourth Regional Plan from 2017 focused on improving regional mass transit, affordable housing, and addressing climate change (Steinberg, 2014).

In the late 1920s and early 1930s, the PANYNJ completed four bridges connecting Staten Island and New Jersey: the Goethals Bridge (opened in 1928) and the corresponding Outerbridge Crossing (named after Eugenius Harvey Outerbridge, the first head of the Port of New York Authority; also opened in 1928), the Bayonne Bridge (opened in 1931), and the George Washington Bridge (connecting Manhattan and New Jersey, opened in 1931; Melosi, 2020; Steinberg, 2014). It also added the Holland Tunnel, the world's first mechanically ventilated vehicular underwater crossing, to its portfolio in 1930/1931 and built the first tube of the Lincoln Tunnel (connecting Manhattan and New Jersey and opened in 1937, later followed by two additional tubes; Doig et al., 2013). In 1958, the Authority started constructing the Elizabeth Marine Terminal in Elizabeth, New Jersey, which served as the prototype for newly invented container shipping that utilized automation, resulting in far fewer workers and worker injuries (called "longshoremen's coffins") and much faster transit times and benefitting from a sustainable rail-freight connection to the nation (Freeman, 2000; Hum, 2014, p. 50; Manbeck, 2004). Thus, New York City's port facilities went defunct, while those in Elizabeth and Newark continue to be among the most hospitable and functional on the entire Atlantic seaboard (Fitch, 1993).

Since the 1950s, the Authority has built or expanded the two larger port terminals in Newark and Elizabeth and smaller port facilities in Hoboken, Brooklyn, and Staten Island. The Authority also built or expanded three major airports: Newark Liberty International (opened in 1928), LaGuardia (opened in 1939 and renamed in 1953), and John F. Kennedy International (opened in 1948 and renamed in 1963), which are the Authority's largest net revenue generating structures. It also built or expanded a small airfield in Teterboro, New Jersey, and the Manhattan Heliport; six interstate bridges and tunnels; two bus terminals in Manhattan; and built and rebuilt the World Trade Center, among many other projects (Doig et al., 2013). The attack on the World Trade Center on September 11, 2001 destroyed the Authority's second-largest net revenue generating structure (Sagalyn, 2016).

The Authority's current portfolio includes the region's three major airports; New Jersey's marine terminals in Port Newark, Port Jersey, Howland Hook, and Red Hook; the region's bridges and tunnels (including the George Washington Bridge and the

Lincoln and Holland tunnels); and the Port Authority Trans-Hudson (PATH) railroad, which connects cities in northeastern New Jersey with Lower and Midtown Manhattan; and most of the land of the World Trade Center (Doig et al., 2013; Shemtob, Sweeney, & Opotow, 2018). The quasi-autonomous and quasi-independent Authority is allowed to float its own bonds, but it does not have the power to tax, thus obtaining its funding from tunnel and bridge toll revenues and airport parking lot fees, among others (Halle & Beveridge, 2013).

The Authority's diverse portfolio has many advantages and some disadvantages. On the one hand, its diversity helps cross-subsidize those venues that operate at a loss, such as the marine terminals and PATH, with others that operate at a profit (Doig et al., 2013). On the other hand, the diversity means that the Authority must balance priorities and resources across its many competing constituencies (Doig et al., 2013). The Authority is designed to be insulated from external political pressures, enabling it to follow its own priorities instead of depending on public referenda (Doig et al., 2013). However, the Authority has faced enormous internal political pressures because of its dependence on its executive director and 12 unpaid commissioners, six from each state, who are appointed rather than elected by the governors of New York and New Jersey based on their expertise or, in some cases, political preferences, as the governors may also break ties or use their authority to veto powers (Doig et al., 2013; Gregory, 1998). Customarily, New York State's governor appoints the executive director and New Jersey's governor appoints the chairperson of the board of commissioners (Sagalyn, 2016).

The Authority has competed with other U.S. ports on the East Coast for centuries. Indeed, between 2017 and 2019, the PANYNJ raised the Bayonne Bridge, which connects Bayonne, New Jersey, with Staten Island, New York, to enable new cargo ships, such as Panamax, New Panamax, or Neopanamax, which handle up to 20 rows of containers stacked up to nine containers high, to dock in Newark (Halle & Beveridge, 2013; Melosi, 2020). Since 2016, these new cargo ships have traveled through the newly constructed third set of locks of the Panama Canal, which connects the Atlantic and Pacific Oceans (Halle & Beveridge, 2013).

While proximity to water is beneficial for shipping goods out of town, the division of New York City by waterfronts, rivers, and bays creates barriers for rail, car, and bus travel that have gradually been addressed through bridges. The Brooklyn Bridge, built by John Augustus Roebling as one of the greatest engineering projects in the nation, opened in 1883 to connect Manhattan and Brooklyn, which had previously only been connected by dozens of ferries operating on the East River (Bender, 2002; Manbeck, 2004; Mensch, 2018; Woodsworth, 2016). The Williamsburg Bridge has connected Manhattan and Brooklyn since 1903 (Bender, 2002; Macaulay-Lewis, 2021). In 1904, the Interborough Rapid Transit (IRT) Company built the city's first subway line, connecting City Hall to Harlem (Kallick, 2013; Spady, 2020). In the same year, the IRT Company opened the elevated transit line, connecting Manhattan with Queens and costing a nickel fare until 1948 (with subsequent fare increases every few years; Demas, 2000; Metropolitan Transit Authority, n.d.; Plotch, 2020). In 1909, the Manhattan and Queensboro Bridges opened, the former connecting Manhattan and Brooklyn and the latter connecting Manhattan and Queens via Roosevelt Island (named as such in 1973, previously named Blackwell's Island and then Welfare Island in 1921; Bender, 2002; Melosi, 2020; Zukin, 1991). The Brooklyn Rapid Transit Company (BRT) and the Brooklyn–Manhattan Transit Corporation (BMT) transit line opened in 1915 and 1917/1918, respectively, connecting Manhattan and Brooklyn (MacKay, 2013; Melosi, 2020; NYC Urbanism, n.d.; Plotch, 2020). By 1940, these and other lines had been consolidated within the New York City subway system, which facilitated commuting by train (Plotch, 2020; Raskin, 2014). The subway system was later merged into the Metropolitan Transportation Authority (MTA), founded in 1965, which runs subways, buses, and commuter rail lines, making it the largest public transit authority in the United States (Dyja, 2021; Mollenkopf & Sonenshein, 2013).

FURTHER INFORMATION

Berg, B. F. (2018). *New York City politics: Governing Gotham*. Rutgers University Press.

Busà, A. (2017). *The creative destruction of New York City*. Oxford University Press.

Gross, J. S., & Savitch, H. V. (2023). *New York*. Agenda Publishing.

Mollenkopf, J. (Ed.). (2005). *Contentious city: The politics of recovery in New York City*. Russell Sage Foundation.

NEW YORK CITY'S EXCEPTIONALISM

New York City is exceptional because of its history, local boosterism, and Robert Moses, among other factors. In terms of its long history of liberalism and leftism, New York City's exceptionalism is evidenced in its many affordable housing innovations, which began with progressive reformers founding civic associations and housing committees and reformers cleaning up the community, establishing philanthropic model tenement buildings and settlement houses, and lobbying state and local policymakers in a bottom-up approach (Freeman, 2000; Helmreich, 2023; Plunz, 2016).

For example, the New York Association for Improving the Conditions of the Poor (AICP), founded in 1844/1845, tasked its subsidiary with building the Work(ing)men's Home in 1855 as one of the first philanthropic model tenement buildings in New York City (Burrows & Wallace, 1999). The Home was a role model in terms of select physical housing innovations and inspired philanthropists about resident behavior and the level of rental income sufficient to satisfy a desired project goal (Plunz, 2016). New York City's progressive civic associations, committees, and housing reformers lobbied the state legislature and organized design competitions and exhibitions to improve housing conditions (Burrows & Wallace, 1999). The University Settlement Society of New York established the Neighborhood Guild on the Lower East Side, the first settlement house in the United States. Organizational and individual philanthropists, including middle- and upper-income (typically White) female volunteers, served recently arrived low-income (mostly European) immigrants through social, educational, and arts programs.

From the mid-19th century to the early 20th century, New York City's progressive housing reformers, including Lawrence Veiller, Edith Elmer Wood, Catherine Bauer, and Mary Kingsbury Simkhovitch, discussed housing challenges during meetings, authored and published reports, and vigorously lobbied the city to elevate minimum housing standards, reduce site coverage, increase setbacks of buildings, and establish air shafts (Wirka, 1996; Zipp, 2010). Then they scaled up their efforts, successfully lobbying the state legislature to establish Tenement House Committees. Their efforts contributed to a series of state tenement laws between 1867 and 1919. Whereas the earlier tenement laws achieved small changes that were often unenforced, the Tenement House Act of 1901 (also called "New Law") was the first law that introduced higher housing design standards, and it remains the basis of New York City's current low-rise rental regulations.

In 1931, Mary K. Simkhovitch and Helen Alfred organized and co-led a group at Greenwich House in New York City called Public Housing Conference, which included members such as socialist Norman Thomas; founder and leader of the Henry Street Settlement Lilian Wald; writer and social critic Lewis Mumford; housing advocates Louis Pink, Edith Elmer Wood, Clarence Stein, and Rabbi Steven Wise; and U.S. Congressman (and future Mayor) Fiorello LaGuardia (McEvilley, 2007; Oberlander & Newbrun, 1999). That same year, the Public Housing Conference evolved into the National Housing Conference (NHC), a national association in Washington, DC dedicated to ensuring safe, decent, and affordable housing for everyone in the United States (Glantz, 2019; National Housing Conference, n.d.; U.S. Department of Housing and Urban Development, n.d.).

The United Housing Foundation (UHF), formally established in 1951 and dissolved in 1971, was not a foundation in the classic sense but a nonprofit organization that pooled investments from financial institutions, insurance companies, pension funds, and others to support union-financed nonprofit or limited-equity cooperatives. The UHF was the largest builder of cooperative housing in New York City, contributing tens of thousands of housing units, including Co-op City (Ballon & Jackson, 2007c; Baum, 2024).

New York City's exceptionalism is also evidenced by its many labor organizations, including two of the most powerful unions in the garment industry in the 1920s, the International Ladies Garment Workers Union (ILGWU) and the Amalgamated Clothing Workers of America (ACWA), along with the United Workers' Association (UWA), the Jewish National Workers Alliance, and the Yiddishist Cooperative Heimgesellschaft, among many others (Freeman, 2000). New York City's exceptionalism is also evidenced by its many credit leagues, social clubs, fraternal societies, newspapers, debating societies that met in small halls and backroom cafes, choral groups, and small theaters, many of them clustered in the Lower East Side (Foner, 2014). The socialist political movement peaked in the 1920s, then started decreasing in importance due to the Great Depression in the 1930s, World War II in the early to mid-1940s, and political repression led by Senator Joseph McCarthy in the late 1940s and 1950s (Baxandall & Ewen, 2000). Nevertheless, New York City still has a relatively high proportion of union members compared to many other major cities (Berg, 2018; Foner, 2013). All these organizations have worked on improving civil rights, housing, health care, education, and the arts over the past decades (Freeman, 2000).

In terms of New York City's decades-long, vigorous local boosterism, Molotch (1976, p. 309) argued that global and local political, business, real estate, media, and cultural elites compete for urban land parcels (i.e., commodities that may appreciate in value), resulting in cities becoming "growth machines" that compete against each other over time. Growth may occur in terms of population, population density, the labor force, the number of businesses, land development, and the level of financial activity (Molotch, 1976).

In the case of New York City, examples of competing global corporations include Forest City Ratner (active from 1920 to 2018), the Related Group (founded in 1972), and Vornado Realty Trust (established in 1959), among others (Angotti, 2008). Examples of competing local real estate families include the Dursts, the Helmsley-Spears, the LeFraks, the Levitts, the Milsteins, the Roses, the Rudins, the Starretts, the Tishman-Speyers, the Trumps, and the Zeckendorfs (Angotti, 2008; Fainstein, 2001).

Examples of competing local economic development organizations in New York City include the New York City Economic

Development Corporation (NYCEDC; previously the Public Development Corporation), the Partnership for New York City, the Association for a Better New York (ABNY), NYC & Company, the Alliance for Downtown New York, NYC Big Events, and New York City Marketing (NYCM), among many others (Busà, 2017; Sagalyn, 2005). Some of these organizations fuel and sustain New York City's competitive position through public–private partnerships (PPPs), which involve quasi-public entities that enjoy eminent domain powers and access to tax credits, along with exemptions from public accountability and public reports, hearings, and citizen participation (Hum, 2014).

In 1991, New York City established the NYCEDC by restructuring the Public Development Corporation, creating a quasi-independent, nonprofit, local development corporation under contract with the city that acts as a liaison between the private, the public, and the nonprofit sectors. The NYCEDC incentivizes and promotes economic growth through (real estate) company expansion and retention, as well as real estate development through bundling tax abatements, public funding, and site improvements; subsidizes or incentivizes developments; sells city-owned properties to investors; and develops, markets, and manages city-owned properties (Katz & Bradley, 2013; New York City Economic Development Corporation, n.d.a). Subsidies may be paid according to federal, state, and local programs or individually negotiated (Moss, 2017). Examples of major development schemes subsidized by the NYCEDC include Times Square, the Towers of the World Trade Center, the South Street Seaport, One World Trade Center, Hudson Yards, and Pacific Park, among many others (Harvey, 1989).

In the 1960s and 1970s, these stakeholders started addressing the city's worsening image crisis by not only independently boosting but also collectively rebranding the city through several innovative and strategic marketing campaigns that were both explicit and implicit, as well as downtown developments such as convention centers or sports arenas (Bagli, 2013; Birge-Liberman, 2017; Blake, 2020; Brash, 2017; Sanders, 2014). For example, developers built more than 66 million square feet of space in New York City from 1967 to 1973, more than twice the amount that was built in any similar period between 1960 and 1992 (Greenberg, 2008).

These approaches were also implemented through business improvement districts (BIDs), a narrowly defined geographic area in which business and commercial real estate owners create a special-purpose entity under the provisions of state law (Chesluk, 2008). BIDs have been allowed by state law since 1981, allowing many stakeholders to address disinvestment or to supplement local government activities (Zukin, Kasinitz, & Chen, 2016). BIDs are authorized to issue their own bonds, and they may assess and tax themselves over and above the citywide tax rate to improve public safety, address homelessness, construct and maintain sidewalks and lighting fixtures, improve street cleanliness, and brand and market through banners and uniform signage, beautification, landscaping, and festivals, among other activities (Fainstein, 2001; Holtzman, 2021). These activities are typically provided by local governments (Chesluk, 2008). BID boards may consist of owners, tenants, residents, and public officials, reflecting neighborhood stakeholders (Mallach & Swanstrom, 2023; Manshel, 2020). Currently, there are more than 1,000 BIDs in the U.S., including the 125th Street BID in Harlem, established in 1993, and the Bryant Park Corporation in Manhattan, established in 1980 (Hyra, 2008, p. xiv; Venkatesh, 2013).

Until the early 1990s, New York City's well-recognized Times Square was a red-light district that had a variety of cheap adult entertainment options and deli-style restaurants (Eng, 2022; Fagan & MacDonald, 2013). In the mid-1990s, Times Square was redeveloped as a clean, tourist-friendly area, with multiplex movie theaters, Madame Tussauds, ABC's Times Square Studios, Hershey's and M&M's stores, and many restaurants, including Planet Hollywood Restaurant and Bar, the Bubba Gump Shrimp Company, Ruby Foo's, and Carmine's, among others (Bender, 2002; Eng, 2022; Fagan & MacDonald, 2013). Thus, some argue that Times Square now feels like Disney World (Dyja, 2021).

The NYCEDC also administers the New York City Industrial Development Agency (NYCIDA), a public benefit corporation created under New York State law in 1974 that assists economically sound businesses that move to or expand within New York City, with property tax abatements for up to 25 years, reduced mortgage recording taxes, and waived city and state sales taxes for purchases of materials and equipment related to construction, all financed by their issued bonds (New York City Industrial Development Agency, n.d.). New York City's mayor appoints the majority of NYCIDA's board, influencing the Agency (Berg, 2018).

New York City also established the nonprofit organization Partnership for New York City, which in 2002 absorbed the New York Chamber of Commerce, founded in 1768 and considered the voice of the business community on economic and social issues and consisting of preeminent business leaders and the employers of more than 1.5 million New Yorkers (Hood, 2017; Steinberg, 2014). The Partnership for New York City is the successor of the New York City Partnership (NYCP), founded in 1979 by financier David Rockefeller, to encourage business leaders to directly collaborate with government and other civic groups, addressing economic and social challenges, promoting local businesses, and connecting the leaders of global industries and government through economic development in four areas: civic engagement and corporate responsibility, education and workforce development, innovation, and transit and infrastructure (Katz & Bradley, 2013; Partnership for New York City, n.d.; Sagalyn, 2005).

The Association for a Better New York (ABNY) was a booster group of real estate developers, bankers, and corporate executives in finance, advertising, market research, retail, tourism, and advertising affiliated with New York City's Convention and Visitors Bureau (CVB). Pursuing funding for the development of Manhattan office towers and hotels, the group attempted to address the exodus of corporations and the decreasing number of visitors caused by the city's image crisis (Holtzman, 2021). On the one hand, the ABNY pursued behind-the-scenes networking, lobbying, and socializing while, on the other, it aggressively used media and marketing to promote the city as a business-friendly town (Phillips-Fein, 2017). For example, ABNY privately accessed public officials and other movers and shakers at the federal, state, and local levels to negotiate tax abatements, eliminate rent control, and build a major convention center while it also worked behind the scenes to prevent late-night talk-show hosts from making jokes about New York City's poor quality of life in their monologues (Greenberg, 2008). The ABNY launched The Big Apple, New York City's first marketing campaign, in 1971. It used many superlatives in its media campaign, distributed golden apple lapel pins and cloth stickers to people all over the city, and cleaned sidewalks and streets in front of corporate headquarters (Greenberg, 2008).

The Big Apple campaign was followed by the city's celebration of the Bicentennial and the 1976 Democratic National Convention, including a statewide blockbuster campaign with the iconic "I ♥ New York" designed by Milton Glaser that was launched during the city's fiscal crisis in 1977 by the New York State Department of Commerce. Further branding efforts included the opening of the two Towers of the World Trade Center in 1973 (Greenberg, 2008). In "Project Appleseed," traveling executives dispensed symbolic New York gifts, such as grass plucked from Central Park, a thread of the Radio City Music Hall curtain, or an envelope of apple seeds from upstate New York (Phillips-Fein, 2017). Other efforts included "New York Stronger than Ever," started a few years after the attack on the World Trade Center; "Just Ask The Locals," launched in August 2007 to focus on the five boroughs and try to get New Yorkers to be nicer to tourists; "This is New York City," launched in October 2007; "Get More NYC: Lower Manhattan," started in 2011; and "Welcome to New York City," launched by Taylor Swift in 2014 (Moss, 2017). These campaigns were popularized through savvy newspaper, magazine, and billboard ads; television and radio commercials; posters; city and lifestyle magazines; and consumer guides; as well as through the sale of New York City-themed accessory items such as t-shirts, mugs, stickers, lapel pins, and pens. Even songs of the several eras, including Frank Sinatra's "New York, New York" and Alicia Keys and Jay-Z's "Empire State of Mind," traded on the theme that the city was a spirited place that compelled visitation (Beveridge & Beveridge, 2013).

Indeed, New York City (or other cities pretending to be New York City) has served as a setting for more hit movies than any other city for every decade in the 20th and 21st centuries except the 1920s, when Paris was featured in nine hit movies (Halle, Vanstrom, Reiff, & Nitschke, 2013). Examples of Manhattan-based hit movies are *Superman* (1978), *Superman 2* (1981), *Superman 3* (1983), *Ghostbusters* (1984), *Spider-Man* (2003), *Spider-Man 2* (2004), and *Spider-Man 3* (2007). Television shows, such as *Sesame Street* (since 1969), *Seinfeld* (1989 to 1998), *Friends* (1994 to 2004), *Sex and the City* (1998–2004), *How I Met Your Mother* (2005–2014), and *Suits* (2011–2019), among many others, have helped perpetuate the city's image as an urbane metropolis populated by smart and funny people where Jane Jacobs-esque chance encounters happen on street corners and in diners and coffee shops (Beveridge & Beveridge, 2013). In the 2000s and early 2010s, Mayor Michael Bloomberg (2002–2013) celebrated and marketed New York City as "a high-end product, maybe even a luxury product [and stated that] New York offers tremendous value, but only for those companies able to capitalize on it" (Bloom, 2015, p. 110; Cardwell, 2003, n.p.; Loughran, 2017). Examples of global signature events are Christo's and Jeanne-Claude's The Gates in Central Park in February 2005, in orange to match the barren trees, and Olafur Eliasson's man-made waterfalls placed along the East River in 2008 (Dyja, 2021; Zukin, 2010).

NYC & Company is a nonprofit quasi-agency that serves as the official destination marketing organization (DMO) and CVB focused on marketing, tourism, and partnerships in New York City (NYC & Company, n.d.a). It has almost 2,000-member organizations and its mission is to maximize travel and tourism opportunities, build economic prosperity, and promote the city's image around the world (NYC & Company, n.d.a). In 2019, NYC & Company's budget was almost $40 million, funded by New York City contract funds (about $20 million), member dues (over $5 million), sponsorships (almost $5 million), publications, the website, other income, licensing, and other grants (NYC & Company, n.d.b). In the mid-2000s, Mayor Bloomberg announced the goal of attracting 50 million visitors per year by 2015, and the goal was reached in 2011 (McGeehan, 2016). Thus, Mayor Bill de Blasio increased the goal to 67 million visitors per year by 2021, but the global COVID-19 pandemic prevented that goal from being met (McGeehan, 2016).

The Alliance for Downtown New York is an organization of property owners, commercial tenants, residents, and elected officials that is also the largest BID in New York City, established in 1995 to promote downtown's revitalization and improve its quality of life (Dyja, 2021). It is the successor of the Downtown-Lower Manhattan Association (DLMA), founded in 1960 and headed by David Rockefeller, representing the financial community downtown, which suggested developing the World Trade Center, completed in 1973 and attacked on September 11, 2001, as well as

Battery Park City, started in 1980 (Bender, 2002; Fainstein, 2001; Phillips-Fein, 2017; Sagalyn, 2016).

In terms of local marketing and tourism, influential real estate professionals, CEOs, and hoteliers established New York City's convention and visitors bureau (CVB) in 1934 to attract travel and tourism, such as through the World's Fair in Flushing Meadows in Queens in 1939/1940 and then in 1964/65 (Eng, 2022; Greenberg, 2008; Heathcott, 2023). Most CVBs in the U.S. are supported by local governments as well as the local tourism, retail, entertainment, and real estate industries, and New York City is no exception (Greenberg, 2008). However, in the 1950s and 1960s, an economically diversified New York City primarily relied on its prominent broadcasting, recording, and publishing industries, not its CVB, to boost its image, unlike other cities like Las Vegas, Nevada, and New Orleans, Louisiana (Greenberg, 2008). However, this reliance changed in the mid-1970s, when the city narrowly escaped bankruptcy, and started depending on its many local economic development and marketing and tourism organizations to not only boost but also to brand the city, as exemplified by the book title *Branding New York: How a City in Crisis Was Sold to the World* (Greenberg, 2008).

New York City has not only been exceptional due to its liberalism and leftism and vigorous local civic boosterism but also partly due to Robert Moses, termed "America's greatest builder," who greatly influenced and shaped land use in New York City through his involvement with planning, transportation, architecture, and state and local policy and politics from the 1920s to the 1960s (Bell & de-Shalit, 2011, p. 253). Moses' work was based on Le Corbusier's visionary, radiant, automobile-centric city with a massive, symbolic downtown that included high-rise office towers and many vast arts and culture facilities, all surrounded by rings of residential suburbs connected through arterial highways in order to reflect the *zeitgeist* of the 1920s (Greenberg, 2008).

As a larger-than-life modernist and activist, Robert Moses had a decades-long reputation as an effective, productive, efficient, and publicity-conscious administrator who served as an intermediary between the government and private investors (Caro, 1974). He planned in advance, accomplished results at record speed, and was well-regarded by many businesses, universities, cultural institutions, public administrators, middle- and high-income homeowners, suburbanites, and tourists (Ballon, 2007). Some compared him to Baron Haussmann, who implemented a massive urban renewal program with grand boulevards, parks, and public works in Paris in the 19th century (Fishman, 2007). Indeed, some called Moses "both an avatar of technocratic city planning and a leading translator of modernist urbanism into the terms of American culture and politics" (Smart, 2017, pp. 46/47).

Moses pursued three goals to strengthen the primacy of New York City's center within its expanding metropolitan region. First, retain existing middle-income (non-Hispanic White) people, including teachers, nurses, municipal employees, and garment workers, and re-attract those who had migrated to the suburbs by offering them modern, attractive, and affordable housing, shopping centers, and cultural facilities. Second, solidify New York City as a center of higher education by providing land for university campus expansions. Third, elevate New York City's local, regional, national, and international stature by building world-class cultural and institutional facilities, such as the United Nations Headquarters and the Lincoln Center for the Performing Arts, which was built on the site of the San Juan Hill neighborhood, displacing hundreds of residents, and was the largest performing arts venue in the country on its opening (Dyja, 2021; Zipp, 2010). Over more than three decades, Moses orchestrated a pro-growth coalition of real estate developers, bankers, insurance companies, and government units, including planners, universities, hospitals, some foundations (for example, the Ford Foundation and the UHF), and some civic groups (for example, the Citizens' Housing and Planning Council; Osman, 2011).

Moses accumulated power throughout his career by obtaining and holding an unprecedented number of administrative offices simultaneously, although he was never elected to public office (Melosi, 2020). He obtained a BA from Yale College in 1909, a BA in Jurisprudence in 1911 and an MA specializing in public administration in 1913, both at Oxford University, and a Ph.D. in political science at Columbia University in 1914 (Melosi, 2020; Schwartz, 2007). In 1914, Mayor John Purroy Mitchell appointed Moses as head of the newly established Civil Service Commission, which pursued local government reform (Caro, 1974). In the early 1920s, the number of work hours decreased for many workers, leading to free Saturdays (not only free Saturday afternoons), while car ownership increased, making open space increasingly important to many people (Caro, 1974). Thus, many New Yorkers started exploring new destinations in the countryside on weekends, while many Long Islanders tried to protect their land, properties, and private roads and beaches, leading to huge traffic jams and visitors having difficulties finding open space for recreation activities (Caro, 1974).

In 1924, Governor Alfred E. Smith appointed Moses as President of the Long Island State Park Commission, where he served until 1962 (Schwartz, 2007). In 1927, Governor Smith appointed Moses as New York's Secretary of State (Caro, 1974). In 1929, Moses became head of the New York Park Association's Metropolitan Conference on Parks (New York City Parks, n.d.). In 1933, Governor Herbert H. Lehman appointed Moses to the State Emergency Public Works Commission, which determined which public projects should be submitted to the Reconstruction Finance Corporation (Caro, 1974; Gutfreund, 2007). Next, Mayor Fiorello LaGuardia appointed Moses as first Commissioner of New York City's Department of Parks in 1934, based on Moses' previous condition of taking the job to consolidate the five separate borough park departments (Howard, 2013). In 1948, Mayor O'Dwyer appointed Moses as chairman of the Mayor's Committee on Slum Clearance, and in 1954, Mayor Robert Wagner reappointed him as Commissioner of New York City's Department of Parks and member of the City Planning Commission (CPC) and appointed him as City Construction Coordinator (Bloom, 2008).

From 1936 to 1964, Moses served as Chairman of the New York State Council of Parks, where he planned the Long Island parkway system, based on the 1929 New York Regional Plan, and the 1939/1940 New York World's Fair, among many other projects (Copquin, 2007; Gutfreund, 2007). Moses headed the Triborough Bridge Authority (TBA) and the New York City Tunnel Authority, both founded in 1933, and then served on the merged Triborough Bridge and Tunnel Authority (TBTA) from 1946 to 1968 (Bloom & Lasner, 2016b; Gregory, 1998; Gutman, 2007). Furthermore, from 1946 until 1960, he served as Chairman of the Mayor's Slum Clearance Committee (SCC), which included heads of municipal departments, New York City Housing Authority (NYCHA), the CPC, the Board of Estimate (BoE, which was responsible for many local policy decisions until 1989), the Department of Buildings, the Comptroller, and the Corporation Counsel (Ballon & Jackson, 2007a, 2007b, 2007c; Melosi, 2020). Moses also oversaw the construction of the 1964/1965 World's Fair from 1960 to 1964 as his last appointment (Biondi, 2007).

Moses' portfolio encompassed projects he was directly responsible for, others where he played a partial role, and yet others where his involvement was minor. His portfolio consisted of many long-term infrastructure projects, including the Brooklyn-Queens, Van Wyck, Major Deegan, Sheridan, Bruckner, Gowanus, Prospect, Whitestone, Clearview, Throgs Neck, Nassau, Staten Island, Long Island, and Cross Bronx expressways; 416 miles of parkways, such as the Henry Hudson Parkway; and 13 bridges, including the Triborough Bridge (renamed the Robert F. Kennedy Bridge in 2008), Verrazano, Throgs Neck, Marine Parkway, Henry Hudson, Cross Bay, and Bronx–Whitestone bridges, and two hydroelectric dams (Gregory, 1998; Heathcott, 2023; Manbeck, 2004; Melosi, 2020). He was also involved with landmarks such as the United Nations, Lincoln Center, Shea Stadium, and campuses for Long Island University, Fordham University, and the Pratt Institute; 1,082 residential buildings with about 148,000 units, including Stuyvesant Town and Peter Cooper Village; more than a dozen beaches; swimming pools; 658 playgrounds; 658 state and city parks; golf courses; and water, sewer, and dock facilities (Larson, 2013; Melosi, 2020; Tippins, 2013).

While 29 states did not have a single state park and six had only one in the 1920s, Moses planned and built a system of state parks from 1923 to 1929 consisting of 45% of all state parks in the nation, including Jones Beach State Park, the first state park, less than 25 miles from Times Square, which was extremely popular with heat-wary New Yorkers for many decades (Caro, 1974; Melosi, 2020). Most expressways are traffic arteries that allow cars and trucks to run through densely populated cities, most parkways (i.e., "ribbonlike parks with landscaped roads within them") only allow cars to run through thinly populated suburbs or the open countryside, providing nice scenery (Gutfreund, 2007, p. 86). In the 1950s and 1960s, most major U.S. cities had expressways on their drawing boards, translating into the displacement of thousands of residents (Caro, 1974). Right after World War II, Moses started building six expressways in New York City simultaneously, culminating in 13 expressways totaling 130 miles by the end of his long career in 1968 (Caro, 1974).

To finance these projects, Moses took advantage of the Public Works Administration (PWA), which was active from 1935 to 1944; the Works Progress Administration (WPA), which operated from 1935 to 1943; the U.S. Housing Act of 1937; the New York State Insurance Code amended in 1938; the (local) Redevelopment Companies Law (RCL); and the U.S. Housing Acts of 1949 and 1954 (Bender, 2002; Gregory, 1998). Moses also collected user fees from toll booths at new roadways, among other sources, and secured financing through newly established public authorities that sold bonds, which do not require voter approval and have less oversight and accountability, unlike the cumbersome and unpredictable ballots to take on debts, subject to strained state and municipal budget limits (Gutfreund, 2007). These public authorities included the Triborough Bridge Authority, which collected toll revenues to fund and maintain the project, and the Triborough Bridge and Tunnel Authority, which Moses first established. Then Mayor Fiorello LaGuardia combined the Triborough Bridge Authority and the New York City Tunnel Authority after the latter had run out of funds partway through the construction of the Queens Midtown Tunnel (Gregory, 1998; Gutfreund, 2007; Heathcott, 2023).

Moses advocated building an efficient, modern metropolis with private developers who could adequately satisfy the housing needs of middle- and upper-income residents (Bloom & Lasner, 2016b; von Hoffman, 2003). These developments benefited from him taking advantage of several public programs, his authority to float bonds, and his championing of the slab block "towers in the park" approach to modernist urbanism, with its slab block, highrise, elevator buildings surrounded by open space (Fainstein, 2010). This design approach was typically utilized for larger projects undertaken by larger developers and builders (Plunz, 2016). Due to Moses' efforts from 1948 to 1960, New York City nominally obtained $65.8 million (about $710 million in 2020 dollars) in Title I funding, more than twice as much as Chicago, which nominally received $30.8 million (about $332 million in 2020 dollars; Ballon,

2007). However, in proportion to population size, New York City (about 7.84 million people in 1950 and about 7.78 million in 1960) received about the same amount of Title I funding as Chicago (about 3.62 million people in 1950 and about 3.55 million in 1960).

Outcomes of U.S. urban renewal in the 1950s and 1960s included the number of substandard housing units and displacements through demolition, and possibly the number of newly constructed units. In terms of the number of substandard housing units, some scholars have stated that the number of substandard units remained the same, while others have stated that the number of substandard units decreased, possibly because of changed definitions of how to count them, residents moving to the suburbs, and the possible success of housing programs implemented in the 1950s and 1960s (Caro, 1974; Gregory, 1998; Plunz, 2016).

In terms of displacement, many people criticized Moses for displacing more than 100,000 residents, many of whom were low-income and of color, as well as small business owners, causing "root shock" (i.e., trauma due to the destruction of one's emotional ecosystem at the individual level) and contributing to residential racial segregation (Fullilove, 2005, p. 11; Metropolitan Council on Housing, n.d.). Moses pursued a "bulldozer approach" across superblocks without public participation and without taking any personal responsibility, but this approach contributed to increased and increasing public opposition and in particular to displacement (Hock, 2016). While Title I required municipalities to relocate displaced residents "in a considerate, human manner," the Committee on Slum Clearance manipulated relocation statistics and did not monitor Title I development corporations (Caro, 1974, p. 965; Gregory, 1998). Thus, many people either moved to dilapidated homes that had been subdivided to accommodate additional in-movers or moved to single room occupancy (SRO) buildings, which typically have private rooms with shared bathroom and kitchen facilities (Farber, 2007). Sometimes displaced people relocated several times or became homeless (Collins & Staff of the New York City Rent Guidelines Board, 2020; Ford, 1994, 2009). Moses justified his activities by stating that he was following prevailing market conditions (Ballon, 2007). While NYCHA allowed displaced residents to return to newly constructed developments, only a very small number and proportion did so (Bloom & Lasner, 2016b). Moses also opposed union-organizing activities (Bell & de-Shalit, 2011).

Moses also had to deal with other defeats. He failed in his bid for governor in 1934 and was unable to gain formal control of NYCHA in 1938 (Gutfreund, 2007). From 1952 to 1958, he tried to build the Lower Manhattan Expressway through Washington Square Park but lost to vocal public opposition led by Shirley Hayes, Jane Jacobs, and other Greenwich Village residents (Fishman, 2007). In the 1950s, Moses also wanted to raze 11 blocks in the Cooper Square neighborhood on the Lower East Side, which would have displaced 2,900 low- and middle-income households, to construct union-sponsored cooperative housing, but he faced fierce community opposition (Anderson, Joseph, & Barnier, 2022; Angotti, 2007; City of New York, 1970; Spicer, Stephens, & Kramer, 2024). In 1959, Frances Goldin founded the Cooper Square Committee, which suggested the Alternative Plan for Cooper Square in 1961 to preserve existing and build new, affordable, low-income housing (Angotti, 2007; City of New York, 1970; Spicer et al., 2024). Between 1968 and the 1990s, the City first adopted and then implemented this Plan (Angotti, 2007; City of New York, 1970). Occasionally, Moses lost some internal battles about exact routes and boundaries (Gutfreund, 2007).

Moses' reputation started declining in the early 1950s, when some professionals started questioning his secretive selection of sites and sponsors, his limited vetting of redevelopment companies, the lack of an established or transparent bidding process, his privatization of relocation, his autocratic methods, and his opposition to preservation (Ballon, 2007). In 1954, the U.S. Senate Committee on Banking and Commerce investigated the developers of the Manhattantown redevelopment, which had acquired the site in 1951, rented out condemned buildings for a large profit, only cleared a portion of the site by that year, abused the Federal Housing Administration (FHA) mortgage insurance program, and inflated construction estimates to take advantage of increased federal funding, among many other inconsistencies (Ballon & Jackson, 2007c). Although Moses defended private redevelopment and the right to collect rents before demolition, he nevertheless started monitoring redevelopment (Ballon, 2007). In 1960, Mayor Robert F. Wagner conducted a major independent investigation, which found evidence of past corruption in the purchase of land and the use of political influence for private stockholder profit by using Title I funding for slum clearance and community development, including in the West Side Urban Renewal Area in 1956 and Manhattantown in 1957 (Bloom & Lasner, 2016d; Levine, 2016). Thus, Wagner removed Moses from the Mayor's SCC that year.

In 1968, Governor Nelson Rockefeller merged the TBTA with the Metropolitan Transportation Authority (MTA), ousting Moses as chairman (Gutman, 2007). Moses' reputation reached its nadir in 1974, when Robert Caro published his Pulitzer Prize-winning biography *The Power Broker: Robert Moses and the Fall of New York* (Gutfreund, 2007). However, some argue that Moses' reputation has risen again since the 1980s, perhaps because his many developments have blended into the urban fabric, suggesting that some albeit not all scars from urban displacement may have healed over time (Ballon & Jackson, 2007a, 2007b, 2007c).

In sum, over the past two centuries, New York City, and in particular Manhattan, has enjoyed exceptionalism in terms of land use. New York City's location on the Atlantic seaboard and the Hudson River has shaped local and regional economic development over time. Since the mid-20th century, New York City has enjoyed premier status among global and major cities due to its enormous concentration of capital and culture, as well as its varied and resilient economy. Over the past few decades, New York City has transitioned from blue-collar manufacturing, influenced by strong labor unions, to a knowledge-based economy (Freeman, 2000). In the mid- to late 1970s, New York City's municipal fiscal crisis decreased the city's liberal redistributive New Deal and managerialist approaches and increased neoliberal and entrepreneurialist approaches, increasing the polarization of the labor and housing markets. Also, New York City has been the quintessential U.S. immigrant city, with high racial and ethnic diversity. It has also had strong and long-term local planning and development efforts.

FURTHER INFORMATION

Anderson, K. (Director, Producer), Joseph, R. (Director, Producer), & Barnier, K. (Director, Producer, Editor). (2022). *Rabble rousers: Frances Goldin and the fight for Cooper Square* [Film]. New Day Films.

Angotti, T. (with Jagu, C.). (2007). *Community Land Trusts and low-income multifamily rental housing: The case of Cooper Square, New York City.* https://etd723z5379.exactdn.com/app/uploads/2024/04/angotti-wp07ta1.pdf

Angotti, T. (2008). *New York for sale: Community planning confronts global real estate.* The MIT Press.

Bagli, C. V. (2013). *Other people's money: Inside the housing crisis and the demise of the greatest real estate deal ever made.* Plume.

Ballon, H., & Jackson, K. T. (Eds.). (2007a). *Robert Moses and the modern city: The transformation of New York.* W. W. Norton & Company.

Caro, R. (1974). *The power broker: Robert Moses and the fall of New York.* Vintage Books.

NEW YORK CITY'S FIVE BOROUGHS
Brooklyn, Manhattan, the Bronx, Queens, and Staten Island

New York City consists of five boroughs, established in 1897 through the New York City Charter, which determines the basic structures of government, including the roles and responsibilities of each official and the government's significant processes, and consolidated in 1898 (Baxandall & Ewen, 2000; Melosi, 2020). The consolidation of 96 governmental units of the five boroughs instantly doubled the population to about 3.5 million, which was more than Paris (about 2.5 million residents) or Chicago (about 1.6 million residents), but less than London (about 6 million residents), and it increased New York City's area from 23 to over 300 square miles (Azzarone, 2022; Melosi, 2020; Revell, 2003). Interestingly, New York City did not pursue comprehensive regional planning, instead limiting its role to zoning, as seen in the 1916 Building Zone Resolution (Angotti, 2008). Nevertheless, the nonprofit RPA, headed by banking and business executives and funded by their affiliated foundations and corporations, introduced the *Regional Plan of New York and its Environments* in 1929, as already discussed in Chapter 7.

New York City's boroughs are Brooklyn (Kings County), Manhattan (New York County), Queens (Queens County), the Bronx (Bronx County), and Staten Island (Richmond County; Quinn, 2022). Some label Brooklyn, Queens, the Bronx, and Staten Island as the "outer boroughs" (Burrows & Wallace, 1999). The five boroughs are all different in terms of demographic, socioeconomic, and housing factors, among others. As of this writing, Brooklyn has almost 30% (almost 1,034,000) of the city's housing units and the highest number of people among all the boroughs (City of New York, n.d.a; New York City Housing Authority, 2022). In the early 19th century, Brooklyn experienced rapid population growth, from 1,603 in 1790, to 4,402 in 1810, to 7,175 in 1820, to 24,592 in 1835, and to 96,838 in 1850 (Steinberg, 2014). In 1855, Brooklyn annexed Williamsburg, Bushwick, and Greenpoint and became the third most populous city in the U.S., with a population of 205,250, which exceeded that of Philadelphia (Hood, 207; Steinberg, 2014). Brooklyn had 266,661 residents in 1860, 396,099 in 1870, about 570,000 in 1880, 800,000 in 1890, and almost 900,000 in 1894, more than Boston, Chicago, St. Louis, or San Francisco (Osman, 2011). This rapid population growth was triggered by Brooklyn's manufacturing industry, making it the fourth largest industrial city in the country in the late 19th century (Woodsworth, 2016). In 1900, Brooklyn had 45 breweries, the highest number of any city in the entire United States (Manbeck, 2004).

Brooklyn's population increased, first rapidly and then gradually, in the early 20th century. In 1920, 1930, 1940, and 1950, it had slightly more than 2 million, more than 2.5 million, almost 2.7 million, and slightly more than 2.7 million people, respectively, facilitated by the Brooklyn Bridge, which connected Brooklyn with Manhattan (Bender, 2002; Macaulay-Lewis, 2021; Melosi, 2020; Raskin, 2014). However, Brooklyn's urbanization took relatively long and started early, about 50 years before the Bronx's urbanization, facilitated by several constructed bridges, including the Third Avenue Bridge (1898), the Willis Avenue Bridge (1901), the University Heights Bridge (1908), and the Madison Avenue Bridge (1910). Interestingly, Brooklyn's urbanization ended late, well after the Bronx's urbanization had peaked (Bender, 2002; Plunz, 2016). Brooklyn has distinct neighborhoods and a unique architectural heritage, with many brownstones (Osman, 2011). Brooklyn's waterfront from Greenpoint to South Brooklyn was the location of many factories specializing in glass, porcelain, cast iron, and pharmaceutical production; printing; sugar and petroleum refining; and brewing from the 1860s to the 1890s, providing jobs for about 260,000 and 110,000 workers, respectively (Rosenberg, 2014). Until the early 2000s, many sugar, coffee, flour, and tobacco warehouses dotted Brooklyn's waterfront (Shepard & Noonan,

2018). In the early 20th century, after World War II, Brooklyn underwent racial and ethnic change. Until the beginning of World War I, it had the largest concentration of Jews (Pritchett, 2002). Many homeowners converted their brownstones to apartment houses (Spady, 2020; Thabit, 2003). In 1948, Brooklyn had the oldest housing stock in the entire city, with almost 90% built before 1920 and almost 65% built before 1899, most of them dilapidated and about one-third either in need of major repairs or lacking private baths (Osman, 2011).

In the late 1940s, 1950s, and 1960s, Brooklyn experienced rapid racial change from majority White to majority Black/African American facilitated by redlining, which is the systematic denial of services, including originating mortgages, as well as other scare tactics such as blockbusting, where unscrupulous realtors convince non-Hispanic White homeowners to sell their homes due to fear of in-moving Blacks/African Americans while also persuading Blacks/African Americans to move to the vacated homes (Anacker, 2024; Thabit, 2003). In the 1960s, Brooklyn gradually started to gentrify, gradually escaping its reputation as a place with Dickensian factories and a physically challenged housing stock worth leaving (Howe, 2010). Currently, Brooklyn is home to many Caribbeans, Russians, Orthodox Jews, and African Americans (Manbeck, 2004).

Brooklyn is famous for Ebbets Field, where the Brooklyn Dodgers invited Jackie Robinson to play first base in 1947, contributing to the World Series championship in 1955 (Manbeck, 2004). Other famous establishments are Junior's Restaurant, Nathan's in Coney Island, the Peter Luger Steakhouse in Williamsburg, and Kleinfeld's Bridal Shop in Bay Ridge, among others (Bender, 2002; Manbeck, 2004).

Manhattan (New York County) is the smallest (in terms of land size) but densest (in terms of population) borough and is currently home to most of the city's skyscrapers, national and international business centers, jobs, amenities, and cultural attractions, as well as containing about 25% (about 878,000 units) of the city's housing stock (City of New York, n.d.a). Writer Kurt Vonnegut labeled Manhattan "Skyscraper National Park" (Melosi, 2020, p. 18). In 1820, Manhattan's population was 124,000, before rapidly increasing to 167,000 in 1825, 197,000 in 1830, 270,000 in 1835, and 313,000 in 1840 (Burrows & Wallace, 1999). In 1865, more than

500,000 New Yorkers lived in 15,000 tenements in Manhattan (Zelasnic, 2007), which had a population of about 1.5 million in 1890, while its net population growth was 146,000 from 1915 to 1920 (Gurock, 2019). In 1903, 2.3 million New Yorkers (about two-thirds of the city's population) lived in 82,000 tenements, with 42,000 in Manhattan, housing more than 85% (about 1.6 million people) of the borough (Dolkart, 2016, p. 47).

One of the most-discussed neighborhoods in Manhattan is the Lower East Side, where several immigrant groups formed ethnic clusters in the mid- to late 19th century, including Little Italy, (Manhattan's) Chinatown, *Kleindeutschland* (Little Germany), and Little Odessa, although boundaries shifted over time and some have disappeared altogether (Milambiling, 2023; Ocejo, 2014; Wallace, 2017). Until the end of World War II, the Lower East Side was New York City's most culturally diverse neighborhood (Mele, 2000). For example, from the 1830s to the 1850s, Irish immigrants typically worked in construction, at the port docks as stevedores, dock workers, or shipbuilders or in warehouses and factories (Barr, 2016; Mele, 2000; Shepard & Noonan, 2018). Starting in the 1860s, the Irish moved from the Sixth, Seventh, and Fourteenth Wards on the Lower East Side to further north on the east and west sides of Manhattan (Shepard & Noonan, 2018). German immigrants typically worked in the trades, in warehouses, and in construction (Barr, 2016; Shepard & Noonan, 2018). In the 1850s and 1860s, they started moving from the Seventh, Tenth, and Thirteenth Wards (*Kleindeutschland*) on the Lower East Side to further north in Yorkville on the Upper East Side of Manhattan in the 1870s and then later to Brooklyn (Helmreich, 2020). In the late 1860s and 1870s, German and Irish immigrants constructed many new brick tenements on Manhattan's Lower East Side, Greenwich Village, along the East River north of East Harlem, and along the Hudson River up to Columbus Circle (Dolkart, 2016). Some of these immigrants served as housing providers (and in some cases as head janitors) after they finished the construction (Sharman, 2006).

Starting in the 1870s, Italians, who typically worked physically demanding jobs in slaughterhouses, breweries, gasworks, coal yards, construction sites, and ironworks next to the port (then called Little Italy), but also worked in tailor shops, barber shops, and as shoemakers or carpenters, replaced the Irish (Maffi, 1995;

Wallace, 2017). There were also highly educated immigrants from Central and Eastern Europe, trained in real estate, entrepreneurship, trading, crafting (including carpentry, shoemaking, painting, and butchering), retailing (including jewelry, watches, and leatherworks), and garment making, who emigrated from their origin countries in 1882 because of the May Laws that prevented them from owning land, farming, settling outside of cities, and originating mortgages, among other activities (Eisenstadt, 2016). In New York City, many experienced upward mobility (Jonnes, 2002). In sum, the Lower East Side was one of the largest immigrant enclaves in the world in the 1870s and 1880s (Wallace, 2017).

In the early 20th century, the Lower East Side had a high proportion of low-income residents (Jonnes, 2002). In 1910, when the Lower East Side reached its population peak, 3% of the entire U.S. population lived in Manhattan (Mele, 2000). Starting in the 1910s, many incoming immigrants no longer moved to the Lower East Side, and many children of immigrants left to move to higher-quality housing units in the Bronx, Brooklyn, and Queens, facilitated by bridges and public transportation (Baxandall & Ewen, 2000). Many Eastern Europeans, such as Czechs, Hungarians, Poles, and Ukrainians, who had replaced the Germans on the Lower East Side, also eventually started moving to northern Manhattan, the Bronx, Brooklyn, and Queens (Legiardi-Laura, 2007).

The Immigration Act of 1924 resulted in a much lower total number of immigrants overall, a decrease of workers from Southern and Eastern Europe that caused a severe labor shortage in New York City, and a large subsequent decline in housing demand on the Lower East Side (Hum, 2014). This trend resulted in high vacancy proportions of 14% in 1928 and 20% in 1930, also showing the area's decades-long, severe housing challenges (Mele, 2000). In sum, in the early to mid-20th century, the Lower East Side transitioned from a neighborhood with immigrant enclaves to a neighborhood with low-income and public housing, boarding houses (which typically served low-income, single males), lunchrooms, pawnshops, liquor stores, and shooting galleries (Sorkin, 2009).

In the 1940s and 1950s, Puerto Ricans, many of whom were employed in the garment industry, started replacing the Italians, while Blacks/African Americans replaced the Irish on the Lower East Side (Legiardi-Laura, 2007). Puerto Ricans, whose migration peaked in 1953, slightly earlier than most other Hispanic/Latino groups, created a vibrant community with *bodegas* (corner grocery stores), *carnicerias* (butcher shops), and *casitas* (lot gardens with small wooden shacks used for outdoor social gatherings during the warmer months; Mele 2000). However, the Lower East Side was also the site of turf wars between youth gangs, crime, and drug dealing (Mele, 2000).

In the late 1960s and early 1970s, the Lower East Side had increased and increasing proportions of tax-delinquent buildings and homesteaders. Some community activists started calling the "indigenous and struggling" Lower East Side "Loisaida," (Spanglish for "Lower East Side"), reflecting the 45% and 69% Hispanics/Latinos who resided in this community in 1970 and 1980, respectively (Foderaro, 1987, n.p.). At the same time, some speculative developers and builders noticed many rehabilitated homes in adjacent neighborhoods, anticipating a spillover effect to the Lower East Side, whose many in-movers had resulted in artists' studios, eccentric cafes, and experimental theaters (Mele, 2000). Thus, these developers and builders started rehabilitating homes geared towards middle- and higher-income people, and they renamed the "artsy and affluent" area between Avenues A and B and between Houston and 14th Streets to the east of the East Side "Alphabet City," making it more appealing to gentrifiers (Foderaro, 1987, n.p.; Milambiling, 2023).

While almost all cities in the U.S. have a distinct downtown, New York City's situation is unusual. Indeed, Lower Manhattan is the third-largest central business district in the nation, providing a relatively large return on investment for the private sector and the government (Moss, 2005). In 2002, it accounted for 25% of New York City's gross city product and almost 12% of its total number of jobs (Sagalyn, 2016). However, more than 40% of its space was built before World War II, so it often lacks or lags behind when it comes to the sophisticated physical and technological infrastructure necessary to keep and attract companies (Moss, 2005).

Some argue that downtown Manhattan is larger than the area south of Fourteenth Street, actually encompassing the area south of 57th Street, including the Times Square District (with Carnegie Hall, the former Carnegie Deli, with its humongous, iconic pastrami sandwiches [closed in 2016], and the Birdland Jazz Club), the

West Side, Murray Hill, the Flatiron Building, Chelsea, Gramercy, Stuyvesant Town, East Village, Greenwich Village, West Village, SoHo, Little Italy, the Lower East Side, (Manhattan's) Chinatown, Tribeca, Battery Park City, and the Financial District (Bender, 2002; Fainstein, 2001; Hamill, 2004). Others argue that Midtown is New York City's commercial or office center, possibly due to its proximity to Grand Central Terminal and Pennsylvania Stations, which are important transportation centers, and the very high density and possible congestion in southern Manhattan (d'Almeida, 2018; Helmreich, 2018). Others argue that New York City does not have a center or a downtown per se but several important nodal points in Manhattan, such as Wall Street, Midtown, Times Square, and Columbus Circle (Babcock & Larsen, 1990).

In the 1920s and 1930s, Harlem, located in Upper Manhattan north of Central Park and sometimes referred to as "Uptown," the "Capital of Black America," "Black mecca," and "the most famous black neighborhood in all the world," was economically diverse and the economic, intellectual, and cultural center of the Harlem Renaissance, a Black cultural movement that brought together people of different backgrounds, including public intellectual W. E. B. DuBois; civil rights activists Asa Philip Randolph and James Weldon Johnson; poets Langston Hughes, Georgia Douglas Johnson, and Claude McKay; writers James Baldwin, Zora Neale Hurston, Alain Locke, Countee Cullen, Nella Larsen, Gwendolyn Bennett, Jessie Redmon Fauset, Ralph Elison, and Dorothy West; musicians Louis Armstrong, Duke Ellington, Charlie Parker, Dizzy Gillespie, John Coltrane, Roland Hayes, Ella Fitzgerald, Marian Anderson, Paul Robeson, and Charlie Johnson; tap dancer and actor Bill "Bojangles" Robinson; social activist and public intellectual Marcus Garvey; and photographers James Van der Zee and Roy DeCarava, among many others (Cohen, 2019, p. 294; Jackson, 2007a, p. 70; Sawadogo, 2022; Sharman, 2006; Taborn, 2018). Harlem was not only the home of the Black elite but also of many low-income people employed as maids, cooks, and servants (Maurrasse, 2006).

Harlem's 125th Street, renamed Martin Luther King Boulevard in 1984, was the heart of its nightlife area, with theaters, dance halls, lounges, speakeasies, cafes, bars, and legendary jazz clubs, such as the Cotton Club (established in 1923), the Lenox Lounge, the Savoy Ballroom (1926, nicknamed "the home of happy feet"), the Apollo (1934), the Franklin and Lincoln Theaters, the Audubon Ballroom, the Poet's Den Theater, the Harlem Repertory Theatre, the National Jazz Museum, Jazzmobile, and Smalls Paradise Club, among others (Gregory, 1998; Jones & Menschel, 2011; Sawadogo, 2022; Sharman, 2006; Taborn, 2018, p. 40). Harlem was the home of several dances, including the Lindy Hop, Peckin', Truckin', the Suzy Q, and the Congeroo (Taborn, 2018). Most of these entertainment venues were owned by Whites (Maurrasse, 2006). While the Savoy was accessible to Blacks and Whites, the Cotton Club only allowed Black artists, but not dark-skinned Black guests (Gregory, 1998; Osofsky, 1996; Taborn, 2018). However, Small's Paradise was not only Black-owned and -operated but also allowed Black guests (Taborn, 2018). Since 1905, Harlem has also been home of the Schomburg Center for Research in Black Culture (Taborn, 2018).

In the 1920s and 1930s, Harlem was also the destination of many Blacks/African Americans who participated in the Great Migration, resulting in 70% of the population in Harlem being Black/African American in the 1930s, facilitated by the extension of the subway (Taborn, 2018). In the 1930s, Harlem went through the Great Depression, and it experienced civil unrest in 1935, 1943, and 1964 caused by long-standing concerns about the lack of jobs, high-quality affordable housing, and public services and (rumors about) police brutality, while its poverty, homelessness, and overall decline gradually increased, reaching its nadir in the 1970s (Abu-Lughod, 2007a, 2007b).

Central Harlem, which ranges from Central Park at East 96th Street in the south up to 155th Street in the north (CD 11), experienced a population decrease from about 237,000 in 1950 to about 101,000 in 1980, partly due to urban renewal (Beveridge, Halle, Telles, & Dufault, 2013). Its racial and ethnic diversity has changed greatly over time, with its proportion of Blacks/African Americans increasing from 1910 (10%) to 1930 (70%) and 1950 (98%) but then decreasing by 2010 (almost 59%; Halle & Beveridge, 2013). Its proportion of Hispanics/Latinos increased from 1980 (4%) to 2010 (almost 24%), and its proportion of non-Hispanic Whites also increased from 1980 (less than 1%) to 2010 (almost 12%), indicating gentrification (Halle & Beveridge, 2013). Currently, Harlem is home to many French-speaking, West African immigrant communities that hail from Senegal, Mali, Guinea, and Burkina Faso (Sawadogo, 2022).

Since the 1990s, Harlem has experienced the New Harlem Renaissance, also called the "second renaissance" or "twenty-first-century renaissance" or "the fourth Black Renaissance," gradually transitioning from a challenged to a gentrifying neighborhood, where high-income, non-Hispanic White homebuyers are gradually replacing low-income Black/African American residents, facilitated by local rehabilitation and renovation initiatives of over $250 million to stimulate economic development (Gates, 1997; Hyra, 2008, p. xiv; Sawadogo, 2022; Sharman, 2006). More recently, some real estate specialists have started calling the entire area of Central Harlem south of 125th Street "SoHa" (South of Harlem) to give the area more cachet (Helmreich, 2018; Sharman, 2006). Harlem's changes have been vividly described by Camilo José Vergara, an immigrant street photographer from Chile, who re-photographs the same buildings from the exact same vantage point over time, documenting urban decay, as published in *Harlem: The Unmaking of a Ghetto* in 2013 (Vergara, 2013). Some scholars compare Vergara with Jacob Riis, who photographed daily life on the Lower East Side in the 1880s, benefitting from the new flash powder photography that allowed him to take pictures inside dark tenement homes and at night (Bull & Gross, 2023; Podemski, 2024). East Harlem, also called "Spanish Harlem" or "El Barrio," has one of the highest proportions of Puerto Ricans in New York City, making it the center of Puerto Rican culture (Mele, 2000; Sharman, 2006).

The Bronx (Bronx County), the only borough not located on an island, is one of the densest boroughs, taking up 43 square miles (Halle & Beveridge, 2013; Quinn, 2022). In 1890, the Bronx had a population of about 100,000 people (Jonnes, 2002) and was the first borough that had accelerated development along extended rail lines and parkways. It had many piano factories in the South Bronx and many parks in the late 19th and early 20th centuries (Moss, 2017). In 1920, 1930, 1940, and 1950, the Bronx had a population of about 730,000, about 1.2 million, almost 1.4 million, and about 1.45 million people, respectively (Jonnes, 2002; Melosi, 2020). Between 1920 and 1930, only 19% of the about 200,000 houses constructed in the 1920s were one- or two-family cottages or duplexes (Plunz, 2016). In the 1930s, the Bronx had the second-highest absolute number, but the highest density of Jews in the United States (Plunz, 2016).

From the 1950s to the 1980s, the South Bronx was the most infamous slum in the entire nation, evidenced by a national evening television audience witnessing fires lighting up the sky during the World Series game between the New York Yankees and the Los Angeles Dodgers, when broadcaster Howard Cosell *supposedly* exclaimed, "Ladies and Gentlemen, the Bronx is burning!" in October 1977, when several hundred fires were burning (Greenberg, 2008, p. 6; Quinn, 2022). The Bronx is home to Co-op City (discussed in Chapter 8), built from 1968 to 1973, which is the largest cooperatively owned housing complex in the United States, containing 15% of all housing units in New York City (about 527,000; Eisenstadt, 2016; City of New York, n.d.a; Quinn, 2022). Since the mid-1980s, New York City and the private sector have heavily invested in the Bronx, particularly the South Bronx, through New York City's *Ten-Year Housing Plan* (discussed in Chapter 6). In sum, Helmreich (2023, p. xiv) argues that compared to the other boroughs, the Bronx still "feels the grittiest and most authentic," as thousands of buildings have remained in their original state (i.e., they have not become gentrified).

Queens (Queens County), with its 117 square miles, is the largest of the five boroughs (in terms of land size), covering over one-third of New York City's area, including the John F. Kennedy and LaGuardia airports (Heathcott, 2023; Hum, 2021; Melosi, 2020; Plunz, 2016). Its population skyrocketed in the early 20th century, from about 150,000 in 1900 to about 470,000 in 1920, more than 1 million in 1930, almost 1.3 million in 1940, and about 1.55 million in 1950, facilitated by the completion of the (Ed Koch) Queensboro Bridge in 1909 and the East River Tunnels connecting Queens and Manhattan in 1910 (Heathcott, 2023; Melosi, 2020). If Queens had been an independent city in 2000, it would have been the fourth largest in the U.S., after New York City, Los Angeles, and Chicago (Jackson, 2007b). While households in the other four boroughs have New York City as a postal address, households in Queens have Long Island City, Jamaica, Flushing, Far Rockaway, and Floral Park addresses, based on a governmental structure established before New York City's consolidation in 1898, and possibly contributing to the perception of a balkanized place (Eng, 2022; Jackson, 2007b). Unlike Manhattan's streets that run from east to west and its avenues that run from north to south, Queens' (271) streets go from north to south and its 167 avenues go from east to west (StreetEasy, 2018). Manhattan's grid was designed with flexibility to add new or rename existing streets and avenues, but Queens' grid was not (StreetEasy, 2018). For example, between First Avenue and Second Avenue, there are avenues called "First Road," "First Drive," or "First Terrace." Similarly, between First Street and Second Street, there are streets called "First Place," or "First Lane" (StreetEasy, 2018). In other words, these irregularities make it difficult to tell the directions and precise locations of some avenues or streets. Thus, many addresses in Queens include hyphenated numbers that indicate the nearest cross avenue (Heathcott, 2023; StreetEasy, 2018). For example, in the address "31-35 55th Street," the nearest cross avenue is 31st avenue, the building number is 35, and the street is 55th street (StreetEasy, 2018).

Between 1948 and 1956, 83% (62,357) of the units in Queens were constructed by a Federal Housing Administration (FHA)-supported limited-dividend company and limited-equity cooperative developments. At the same time, Queens' housing stock is about 70% single-family homes and duplexes, often surrounded by private yards and labeled the "garden borough" by some (Bloom & Lasner, 2016). Queens was home to jazz legends Louis Armstrong, Count Basie, Ella Fitzgerald, and Lena Horne, among others (Hum, 2021).

Queens' racial and ethnic composition started changing rapidly in the 1970s (Salvo & Lobo, 2021). While non-Hispanic Whites accounted for about 80% of Queens' residents in 1970, Hispanics/Latinos, Asians, and Blacks/African Americans made up 28%, 24%, and 18% (thus 70%) of its residents in 2014 (Salvo & Lobo, 2021). Currently, Queens has 25% (about 851,000) of the city's housing units and is the most diverse borough in New York City in terms of race, ethnicity, and nativity, with high proportions of Black/African American households and immigrants (City of New York, n.d.a; Heathcott, 2023; Hum, 2021; Larson, 2017). Nevertheless, there is high racial and ethnic residential segregation among groups (Hum, 2021).

About 50% of Queens' residents are foreign-born, hailing from more than 120 countries, although there is no single predominant racial or ethnic immigrant group (Hum, 2021; Kallick, 2021; Larson, 2017). Immigrant groups have come from Bangladesh, India, Ecuador, the Dominican Republic, Guyana, among many other nations (Salvo & Lobo, 2021). More than 55% speak a language other than English at home (Heathcott, 2023).

Queens' neighborhoods with the highest immigrant density are Corona, Elmhurst, and Jackson Heights (Gregory, 1998; Hum, 2021). Queens' major urbanization wave began last of all five boroughs (Plunz, 2016), and gentrification has happened sporadically so far (Moss, 2017). In sum, Heathcott (2023) distinguishes Queens from the other four boroughs, pointing out that it lacks Manhattan's nightlife, grand skylines, iconic architecture, and great historic sites; it does not have Brooklyn's dignity and aged charm; it lacks the edginess and renown of the Bronx; and it does not have the separatist fervor of Staten Island.

Finally, Staten Island (Richmond County) is the southernmost borough and is the third largest in terms of land size, the least populous, the least densely populated, and the most geographically separate from the other boroughs, about five miles from Manhattan, with a residential and suburban character and about 5% (almost 179,000 units) of the city's housing stock (City of New York, n.d.a; Melosi, 2020). Staten Island was built on the Fresh Kills Landfill, the municipally owned main repository for the city's residential trash and the largest municipal landfill in the world, operating from 1948 until 2001 (Melosi, 2020; Steinberg, 2014). It is currently being redeveloped as Freshkills Park, which will become New York City's second-largest park, three times the size of Central Park (Campo, 2013; Melosi, 2020). Some feel that Staten Island's character is suburban and that it has a great sense of community, while others perceive it as backwater and provincial, calling it the "forgotten borough," possibly because it is only connected to Manhattan via a ferry crossing the Upper (New York) Bay, not by rail, and because it has only been connected to Brooklyn by express bus routes traversing the Verrazzano-Narrows Bridge since the mid-1960s (Ludwig, 2013, p. 207; Melosi, 2020).

FURTHER INFORMATION

Copquin, C. G. (2007). *The neighborhoods of Queens.* Yale University Press.

Hilderban, G. (Director, Producer), Vazquez, V. (Director, Producer), Martinez, N. (Producer), & Allen, J. (Producer). (2020). *Decade of fire* [Film]. Bayview Entertainment.

Manbeck, J. B. (Ed.). (2004). *The neighborhoods of Brooklyn.* Yale University Press.

Melosi, M. V. (2020). *Fresh Kills: A history of consuming and discarding in New York City.* Columbia University Press.

Woodsworth, M. (2016). *Battle for Bed-Stuy: The long war on poverty in New York City.* Harvard University Press.

CONCLUSION

Over the past few centuries, New York City has been characterized by never-ending change. In the recent past and the near and distant future, New York City will face two major challenges: climate change and socioeconomic inequality. The former is going to impact *all* and the latter is going to impact *many* New Yorkers. Climate change has already been visible through sea-level rise; coastal erosion and coastal storms; an increase in the number, frequency, and intensity of coastal storm surges; high winds; as well as an increase in the number of days above 90 degrees Fahrenheit. While New York City has passed several ambitious strategies, plans, policies, and regulations over the past two decades, including its *PlaNYC 2030: A Greener, Greater New York*, it remains to be seen whether it will meet the goal of reducing 2005 greenhouse gas (GHG) emissions by 30% by 2030 (City of New York, 2007).

Climate change has magnified existing socioeconomic inequalities in the New York metropolitan area which has ranked fairly high in terms of socioeconomic inequality compared to other metropolitan areas in the U.S. Consequences of socioeconomic inequality include challenges in households paying for food, housing, transportation to work, utilities, and child- and health-care expenditures, as well as saving for emergencies, retirement, and other professional and personal pursuits (Sawhill, 2018). Many households affected by inequality tend to be low-income, of color, or both. New York City's socioeconomic inequality was exemplified by the Occupy Wall Street (OWS) movement which started in

2011, a few months after the (technical) end of the Great Recession (Mollenkopf & Sonnenshein, 2013). Over the past few decades, climate change and socioeconomic inequality have been major challenges which New York City has tried to address although the impact of recent changes in federal policies is currently still unclear as of this writing.

New York City has been *demographically* more resilient than many other cities. Its population reached 8.8 million as of April 2020 but it was less than 8.5 million as of March 2025, partly due to the COVID-19 pandemic (City of New York, 2025). Population numbers are not only influenced by births and deaths, which are easier to forecast, but also by domestic and international migration, which are more difficult to estimate. Indeed, the latter two are influenced by access to professional opportunities, personal networks, and the overall local economy. Also, international migration is influenced by federal policy which may be very difficult to predict.

New York City has also been *economically* more resilient than many other cities, faring much better during most recessions except during the one decade-long economic decline in the 1970s (Kinder, 2016; Kirshner, 2019; Medoff & Sklar, 1994). As of this writing, the feared upcoming recession may be less pronounced in New York City than in other large U.S. cities as a disproportionate proportion of its employment is in information, financial activities, and professional and business services (Sambeck, 2025).

New York City has faced a housing affordability crisis for many decades, as evidenced in the relatively high number and proportion of renters who face a relatively high housing cost burden, translating into missing or alternate rental payments, (severely) crowded housing units, and low vacancy rates.

Over the past few decades, many New York City mayors have created long-term housing plans which have put a dent—albeit a massive one—into addressing New York City's affordable housing crisis. In December 2024, City Council passed the zoning reform *City of Yes for Housing Opportunity* (COYFHA), introduced by Mayor Eric Adams in April 2024. Municipal officials estimated that COYFHA may result in about 80,000 new housing units over the next 15 years (Nahmias & Cattan, 2024). COYFHA also addresses parking requirements, based on dividing the city into three tiers, allows conversions from underutilized nonresidential buildings constructed between 1961 and 1991 to housing, reintroduces small housing as well as residences with shared common facilities, and also allows facilitating adding new housing on large "campus" sites with existing buildings, among many other regulations (City of New York, n.d.g; Evelly, 2024; Nahmias & Cattan, 2024). As of this writing, it remains to be seen if, when, and how COYFHA impacts the housing affordability crisis.

In sum, while there may be headwinds ahead, New York City may weather current and future uncertainties better than many other cities. It is going to remain exceptional, partly due to its large number and proportion of passionate and talented, creative people eager to advance their careers and be a part of the collective urban endeavor, civicism, and civic-mindedness for years and decades to come.

REFERENCES

Abu-Lughod, J. (2007a). *Race, space, and riots in Chicago, New York, and Los Angeles.* Oxford University Press.

Abu-Lughod, J. (2007b). Money, politics, and protest: The struggle for the Lower East Side. In C. Patterson (Ed.), *Resistance: A radical political and social history of the Lower East Side* (pp. 79–86). Seven Stories Press.

Adams, S. P. (2014). *Home fires: How Americans kept warm in the 19th century.* Johns Hopkins University Press.

Ali, S. H., Connolly, C., & Keil, R. (2023). *Pandemic urbanism.* Polity.

American Planning Association. (2020). Community Parks Initiative: NYC Parks: 2020 Advancing Diversity and Social Change in Honor of Paul Davidoff. https://www.planning.org/awards/2020/excellence/community-parks-initiative/#:~:text=To%20distribute%20park%20investments%20more,parks%20in%20high%2Dneed%20areas.

Anacker, K. B. (2019). Editorial introduction: Housing affordability and affordable housing. *International Journal of Housing Policy, 19*(1), 1–16.

Anacker, K. B. (2022). U.S. suburbs and the global COVID-19 pandemic: From cleanscapes to safescapes 2.0? The case of the New York metropolitan area. *Urban Geography, 43*(8), 1260–1267.

Anacker, K. B. (2024). *Housing in the United States: The basics.* Routledge.

Anacker, K. B., & Li, Y. (2016). Rental housing affordability of U.S. renters during the Great Recession, 2007 to 2009. *Housing and Society, 43*(1), 1–17.

Anasi, R. (2012). *The last Bohemia: Scenes from the life of Williamsburg, Brooklyn.* Farrar, Strauss and Giroux.

Anderson, K. (Director, Producer), Joseph, R. (Director, Producer), & Barnier, K. (Director, Producer, Editor). (2022). *Rabble rousers: Frances Goldin and the fight for Cooper Square* [Film]. New Day Films.

Anderson, M. (2015, July 14). The Manhattan skyline: Why are there no tall skyscrapers between midtown and downtown? Environmental Protection Agency. https://blog.epa.gov/2015/07/14/the-manhat

tan-skyline-why-are-there-no-tall-skyscrapers-between-midtown-and-downtown/
Angotti, T. (2007). *Community Land Trusts and low-income multifamily rental housing: The case of Cooper Square, New York City.* https://etd723z5379.exactdn.com/app/uploads/2024/04/angotti-wp07ta1.pdf
Angotti, T. (2008). *New York for sale: Community planning confronts global real estate.* The MIT Press.
Angotti, T. (2014, June 12). *A tale of two housing plans: De Blasio's drive to build big undermines neighborhood preservation.* The Indypendent.
Anheier, H. K., Lam, M., & Howard, D. B. (2013). The nonprofit sector in New York City and Los Angeles. In D. Halle & A. A. Beveridge (Eds.), *New York and Los Angeles: The uncertain future* (pp. 513–532). Oxford University Press.
Asch, C. M., & Musgrove, G. D. (2017). *Chocolate city: A history of race and democracy in the nation's capital.* The University of North Carolina Press.
Atkinson, R., & Burrows, R., Glucksberg, L., Ho, H. K., Knowles, C., & Rhodes, D. (2017). Minimum city? The deeper impacts of the "super-rich" on urban life. In R. Forrest, S. Y. Koh, & B. Wissink (Eds.), *Cities and the super-rich: Real estate, elite practices, and urban political economies* (pp. 253–271). Palgrave Macmillan.
Azzarone, S. (2022). *Heaven on the Hudson: Mansions, monuments, and marvels of Riverside Park.* Fordham University Press.
Babcock, R. F., & Larsen, W. U. (1990). *Special districts: The ultimate in neighborhood zoning.* Lincoln Institute of Land Policy.
Bagchee, N. (2018). *Counter institution: Activist estates of the Lower East Side.* Fordham University Press.
Bagli, C. V. (2013). *Other people's money: Inside the housing crisis and the demise of the greatest real estate deal ever made.* Plume.
Baker, T. (2017). The garden on the machine. In C. Lindner & B. Rosa (Eds.), *Constructing the High Line: Postindustrial urbanism and the rise of the elevated park* (pp. 109–124). Rutgers University Press.
Ballon, H. (2007). Robert Moses and urban renewal: The Title I Program. In H. Ballon & K. T. Jackson (Eds.), *Robert Moses and the modern city: The transformation of New York* (pp. 94–115). W. W. Norton & Company.
Ballon, H. (Ed.) (2011a). *The greatest grid: The master plan of Manhattan 1811–2011.* Museum of the City of New York and Columbia University Press.
Ballon, H. (2011b). Introduction. In H. Ballon (Ed.), *The greatest grid: The master plan of Manhattan 1811–2011* (pp. 13–15). Museum of the City of New York and Columbia University Press.
Ballon, H. (2011c). 2. The Commissioners' Plan of 1811. In H. Ballon (Ed.), *The greatest grid: The master plan of Manhattan 1811–2011* (p. 27). Museum of the City of New York and Columbia University Press.

Ballon, H. (2011d). 4. Opening streets. In H. Ballon (Ed.), *The greatest grid: The master plan of Manhattan 1811–2011* (p. 73). Museum of the City of New York and Columbia University Press.

Ballon, H., & Jackson, K. T. (Eds.). (2007a). *Robert Moses and the modern city: The transformation of New York*. W. W. Norton & Company.

Ballon, H., & Jackson, K. T. (2007b). Introduction. In H. Ballon & K. T. Jackson (Eds.), *Robert Moses and the modern city: The transformation of New York* (pp. 65-66). W. W. Norton & Company.

Ballon, H., & Jackson, K. T. (2007c). Housing and urban renewal. In H. Ballon & K. T. Jackson (Eds.), *Robert Moses and the modern city: The transformation of New York* (pp. 242–307). W. W. Norton & Company.

Barr, J. M. (2016). *Building the skyline: The birth and growth of Manhattan's skyscrapers*. Oxford University Press.

Bauer, C. (2020). *Modern housing*. University of Minnesota Press.

Baum, J. (2024). *Just city: Growing up on the Upper West Side when housing was a human right*. Fordham University Press.

Baxandall, R., & Ewen, E. (2000). *Picture windows: How the suburbs happened*. Basic Books.

Befferman, J. (2023, December 27). Mayor Adams announces executive order aimed at restricting Texas Gov. Greg Abbott's migrant busing. https://www.politico.com/news/2023/12/27/adams-executive-order-abbott-migrant-bus-00133250

Bell, D. A., & de-Shalit, A. (2011). *The spirit of cities: Why the identity of a city matters in a global age*. Princeton University Press.

Bender, T. (2002). *The unfinished city: New York and the metropolitan idea*. New York University Press.

Berenyi, E. B. (1989). *Locally funded housing programs in the United States: A survey of the 51 most populated cities*. Community Development Research Center.

Berg, B. F. (2018). *New York City politics: Governing Gotham*. Rutgers University Press.

Beveridge, A. A., & Beveridge, S. J. (2013). The big picture: Demographic and other changes. In D. Halle & A. A. Beveridge (Eds.), *New York and Los Angeles: The uncertain future* (pp. 33–78). Oxford University Press.

Beveridge, A. A., Halle, D., Telles, E., & Dufault, B. L. (2013). Residential diversity and division: Separation and segregation among Whites, Blacks, Hispanics, Asians, affluent, and poor. In D. Halle & A. A. Beveridge (Eds.), *New York and Los Angeles: The uncertain future* (pp. 310–339). Oxford University Press.

Biondi, M. (2007). Robert Moses, race, and the limits of an activist State. In H. Ballon & K. T. Jackson (Eds.), *Robert Moses and the modern city: The transformation of New York* (pp. 116–121). W. W. Norton & Company.

Birge-Liberman, P. (2017). The urban sustainability fix and the rise of the conservancy park. In C. Lindner & B. Rosa (Eds.), *Constructing the High

Line: Postindustrial urbanism and the rise of the elevated park (pp. 125–140). Rutgers University Press.

Blake, A. M. (2020). *How New York became American, 1890–1924*. Johns Hopkins University Press.

Bloom, N. D. (2008). *Public housing that worked: New York in the twentieth century*. University of Pennsylvania Press.

Bloom, N. D. (2015). Myth #4: High-rise public housing is unmanageable. In N. D. Bloom, F. Umbach, & L. J. Vale (Eds.), *Public housing myths: Perception, reality, and social policy* (pp. 91–118). Cornell University Press.

Bloom, N. D., & Lasner, M. G. (2016a). Introduction. In N. D. Bloom & M. G. Lasner (Eds.), *Affordable housing in New York: The people, the places, and policies that transformed a city* (pp. 1–14). Columbia University Press.

Bloom, N. D., & Lasner, M. G. (2016b). Public housing towers. In N. D. Bloom & M. G. Lasner (Eds.), *Affordable housing in New York: The people, the places, and policies that transformed a city* (pp. 113–125). Columbia University Press.

Bloom, N. D., & Lasner, M. G. (2016c). Stabilizing the middle. In N. D. Bloom & M. G. Lasner (Eds.), *Affordable housing in New York: The people, the places, and policies that transformed a city* (pp. 139–150). Columbia University Press.

Bloom, N. D., & Lasner, M. G. (2016d). Housing reimagined. In N. D. Bloom & M. G. Lasner (Eds.), *Affordable housing in New York: The people, the places, and policies that transformed a city* (pp. 193–201). Columbia University Press.

Bloom, N. D., & Lasner, M. G. (2016e). The decentralized network. In N. D. Bloom & M. G. Lasner (Eds.), *Affordable housing in New York: The people, the places, and policies that transformed a city* (pp. 245–257). Columbia University Press.

Bloomberg, M. R. (2011). Reflection. In H. Ballon (Ed.), *The greatest grid: The master plan of Manhattan 1811–2011* (p. 25). Museum of the City of New York and Columbia University Press.

Botein, H., & Hetling, A. (2016). *Home safe home: Housing solutions for survivors of intimate partner violence*. Rutgers University Press.

Bowdler, J., Quercia, R., & Smith, D. A. (2010). *The foreclosure generation: The long-term impact of the housing crisis on Latino children and families*. https://communitycapital.unc.edu/files/2010/02/Foreclosure-Generation.pdf

Brash, J. (2011). *Bloomberg's New York: Class and governance in the luxury city*. The University of Georgia Press.

Brash, J. (2017). Park (In)equity. In C. Lindner & B. Rosa (Eds.), *Constructing the High Line: Postindustrial urbanism and the rise of the elevated park* (pp. 73–91). Rutgers University Press.

Brenzel, K. (2017, May 17). *High construction wages, material costs make NYC the world's most expensive place to build: Report*. The Real Deal.

Brower, B. (1989). *Missing the mark: Subsidizing housing for the privileged, displacing the poor: An analysis of the City's 10-year plan*. The Association for Neighborhood and Housing Development, Inc. and The Housing Justice Campaign.

Burleigh, E. (2024, June 4). New York City is home to most Fortune 500 companies and second place isn't even close. https://finance.yahoo.com/news/york-city-home-most-fortune-110000904.html?guccounter=1&guce_referrer=aHR0cHM6Ly93d3cuZ29vZ2xlLmNvbS8&guce_referrer_sig=AQAAAAP9mNUXaNnsGRO_dN9EmNDrxj9NDcdSbaODzDhrhV9kO6CIc_LnpjPQ1x3c8JClXMcB9y4u_KUXpzEfE8J1OHtIIuhz0uCCbkA_U_qsahzNrTsEnlOfjCzst1lmPxs60PBbNE5C__6_ts8vLw7-E7uI1Z5eticMZeq8-PSdp3HR

Burrows, E. G., & Wallace, M. (1999). *Gotham: A history of New York City to 1898*. Oxford University Press.

Busà, A. (2017). *The creative destruction of New York City*. Oxford University Press.

Caldwell, M. (2005). *New York night: The mystique and its history*. Scribner.

Cammenga, J. (2020, August 26). How high are property taxes in your state? Tax Foundation. https://taxfoundation.org/how-high-are-property-taxes-in-your-state-2020/

Campo, D. (2013). *The accidental playground: Brooklyn waterfront narratives of the undesigned and unplanned*. Fordham University Press.

Capperis, S., de la Roca, J., Ellen, I. G., Karfunkel, B., Kuai, Y., Moriarty, S., Steil, J., Stern, E., Suher, M., Weselcouch, M., Willis, M., & Yager, J. (2014). *State of New York City's housing and neighborhoods in 2014*. https://furmancenter.org/research/sonychan/2014-report

Cardwell, D. (2003, January 8). Mayor says New York is worth the cost. *The New York Times*.

Caro, R. (1974). *The power broker: Robert Moses and the fall of New York*. Vintage Books.

Center on Budget and Policy Priorities. (2019, June 6). *Chart book: The legacy of the Great Recession*. https://www.cbpp.org/research/economy/chart-book-the-legacy-of-the-great-recession

Center Square, The. (2020, June 12). *54 companies headquartered in New York made Fortune 500 list*. https://www.thecentersquare.com/new_york/54-companies-headquartered-in-new-york-made-fortune-500-list/article_7ec552ee-a601-11ea-87f1-2f71d5c2e7b6.html

Central Park Conservancy (n.d.). *Seneca Village site*. https://www.centralparknyc.org/locations/seneca-village-site

Chesluk, B. (2008). *Money jungle: Imagining the new Times Square*. Rutgers University Press.

Chin, M. M. (2005). *Sewing women: Immigrants and the New York City garment industry*. Columbia University Press.

Citizens Housing and Planning Council. (1995, January/February). Giuliani confronts *in rem* dilemma. *The Urban Prospect: Housing, Planning and Economic Development in New York* 1(1), 1, 2, 4.

City of New York. (n.d.a). *2023 NYC Housing and Vacancy Survey (HVS)*. https://www.nyc.gov/assets/hpd/downloads/pdfs/about/2023-nychvs-selected-initial-findings.pdf

City of New York. (n.d.b). *New York City population: Population facts*. https://www1.nyc.gov/site/planning/planning-level/nyc-population/population-facts.page

City of New York. (n.d.c). *Tenant Interim Lease (TIL) Program*. https://portal.311.nyc.gov/article/?kanumber=KA-03052

City of New York. (n.d.d). *Tenant Associations*. https://www1.nyc.gov/site/hpd/services-and-information/tenant-associations.page

City of New York. (n.d.e). *TV/Film*. https://www1.nyc.gov/site/mome/industries/ny-state-tax-credit.page

City of New York. (n.d.f). *2020 Census*. https://www.nyc.gov/site/planning/planning-level/nyc-population/2020-census.page

City of New York. (n.d.g). *City of yes for housing opportunity*. https://storymaps.arcgis.com/stories/f266a53c9cda42d5b7f63b57dc08f849

City of New York. (n.d.h). *Where we live NYC: Confronting segregation and taking action to advance opportunity for all*. https://www.nyc.gov/site/hpd/news/003-23/city-commits-3-1-million-combat-source-of-income-discrimination-reports-progress-made-on#/0

City of New York. (n.d.i). *Community Parks Initiative*. Department of Parks and Recreation. https://www.nycgovparks.org/about/framework-for-an-equitable-future/community-parks-initiative

City of New York. (1970). *Cooper Square Community Development Plan (Urban Renewal Plan)*. https://coopersquare.org/wp-content/uploads/2009/06/csc-1970-alternateplan.pdf

City of New York. (2007). *PlanNYC 2030: A greener, greater New York*. https://www.nyc.gov/html/planyc/downloads/pdf/publications/full_report_2007.pdf

City of New York. (2010). *New Housing Marketplace Plan*. https://courseworks2.columbia.edu/files/661867/download?download_frd=1

City of New York. (2013). *Mayor Bloomberg announces winner of Adapt NYC Competition to develop innovative micro-unit apartment housing model*. https://www1.nyc.gov/office-of-the-mayor/news/032-13/mayor-bloomberg-winner-em-adapt-nyc-em-competition-develop-innovative-micro-unit#/1

City of New York. (2014). *Housing New York: A five-borough, ten-year Plan*. http://www.nyc.gov/html/housing/assets/downloads/pdf/housing_plan.pdf

City of New York. (2017a). *Turning the tide on homelessness in New York City.* https://www.nyc.gov/assets/dhs/downloads/pdf/turning-the-tide-on-homelessness.pdf

City of New York. (2017b). *Housing New York 2.0.* https://www1.nyc.gov/site/housing/about/our-plan.page

City of New York. (2019). *OneNYC 2050: Building a strong and fair city.* http://1w3f31pzvdm485dou3dppkcq.wpengine.netdna-cdn.com/wp-content/uploads/2020/01/OneNYC-2050-Full-Report-1.3.pdf

City of New York. (2020). *State of the city 2020.* https://www1.nyc.gov/office-of-the-mayor/state-of-the-city.page

City of New York. (2021). *Annual report on tax expenditures.* https://www.nyc.gov/assets/finance/downloads/pdf/reports/reports-tax-expenditure/ter_2021_final.pdf

City of New York. (2023). *2023 annual report on New York City's immigrant population and initiatives of the Office.* https://www.nyc.gov/assets/immigrants/downloads/pdf/MOIA-Annual-Report-2023_Final.pdf

City of New York. (2024). *Facts, not fear: How welcoming immigrants benefits New York City.* https://comptroller.nyc.gov/reports/facts-not-fear-how-welcoming-immigrants-benefits-new-york-city/#:~:text=Approximately%20476%2C000%20undocumented%20immigrants%20lived,compared%20to%20504%2C000%20in%202018

City of New York. (2025, March 13). *Mayor Adams celebrates two consecutive years of population growth in New York City.* https://www.nyc.gov/office-of-the-mayor/news/140-25/mayor-adams-celebrates-two-consecutive-years-population-growth-new-york-city

Clergé, O. (2019). *The new noir: Race, identity, and diaspora in Black suburbia.* University of California Press.

Cohen, L. (2019). *Saving America's cities: Ed Logue and the struggle to renew urban America in the suburban age.* Farrar, Straus and Giroux.

Colburn, G., & Walter, R. J. (2025). *Affordable housing in the United States.* Routledge.

Collins, T. L., & Staff of the New York City Rent Guidelines Board (2020). *An introduction to the New York City Rent Guidelines Board and the rent stabilization system.* https://rentguidelinesboard.cityofnewyork.us/about/an-introduction-to-the-nyc-rent-guidelines-board-and-the-rent-stabilization-system/

Copquin, C. G. (2007). *The neighborhoods of Queens.* Yale University Press.

Cromley, E. C. (1990). *Alone together: A history of New York's early apartments.* Cornell University Press.

Currid, E. (2007). *The Warhol economy: How fashion, art, and music drive New York City.* Princeton University Press.

D'Almeida, A. C. (Ed.). (2018). *Smarter New York city: How city agencies innovate.* Columbia University Press.

David, J., & Hammond, R. (2011). *High Line: The inside story of New York City's park in the sky*. Farrar, Straus and Giroux.

Demas, C. (2000). *Eleven stories high: Growing up in Stuyvesant Town, 1948–1968*. State University of New York Press.

Detter, D. & Fölster, S. (2017). *The public wealth of cities: How to unlock hidden assets to boost growth and prosperity*. Brookings Institution Press.

Doig, J. W., Erie, S. P., & Mackenzie, S. A. (2013). America's leading international trade centers and their entrepreneurial agencies. In D. Halle & A. A. Beveridge (Eds.), *New York and Los Angeles: The uncertain future* (pp. 103–133). Oxford University Press.

Dolkart, A. S. (2016). Tenements. In N. D. Bloom & M. G. Lasner (Eds.), *Affordable housing in New York: The people, the places, and policies that transformed a city* (pp. 45–48). Columbia University Press.

Dordick, G. A. (1997). *Something left to lose: Personal relations and survival among New York's homeless*. Temple University Press.

Dyja, T. (2021). *New York, New York, New York: Four decades of success, excess, and transformation*. Simon & Schuster.

Eisenstadt, P. (2016). Abraham Kazan. In N. D. Bloom & M. G. Lasner (Eds.), *Affordable housing in New York: The people, the places, and policies that transformed a city* (pp. 167–170). Columbia University Press.

Ellen, I. G., & Karfunkel, B. (2016). *Renting in America's largest metropolitan areas*. https://furmancenter.org/files/NYU_Furman_Center_Capital_One_National_Affordable_Rental_Housing_Landscape_2016_9JUNE2016.pdf

Eng, A. (2022). *Our laundry, our town: My Chinese American life from Flushing to the Downtown stage and beyond*. Fordham University Press.

Evelly, J. (2024, December 5). What the Council's revamped "City of Yes for Housing" deal includes. https://citylimits.org/2024/12/05/what-the-councils-revamped-city-of-yes-for-housing-deal-includes/

Fagan, J., & MacDonald, J. (2013). Policing, crime, and legitimacy in New York and Los Angeles: The social and political contexts of two historic crime declines. In D. Halle & A. A. Beveridge (Eds.), *New York and Los Angeles: The uncertain future* (pp. 219–262). Oxford University Press.

Fahim, K. (2010, March 21). Despite much rezoning, scant change in residential capacity. *The New York Times*.

Fainstein, S. S. (2001). *The city builders: Property development in New York and London, 1980–2000*. University Press of Kansas.

Fainstein, S. S. (2010). *The just city*. Cornell University Press.

Farber, S. (2007). Homelessness, madness, the power elites and final battles of the East Village. In C. Patterson (Ed.), *Resistance: A radical political and social history of the Lower East Side* (pp. 166–179). Seven Stories Press.

Feagin, J. R. (2016). *How Blacks built America: Labor, culture, freedom, and democracy*. Routledge.

Ferguson, S. (2007). The struggle for space: Ten years of turf battling on the Lower East Side. In Patterson (Ed.), *Resistance: A radical political and social history of the Lower East Side* (pp. 141–165). Seven Stories Press.

Ferré-Sadurní, L. (2024, May 25). Why N.Y.C. hotel rooms are so expensive right now: The average hotel room rate in the city is $301 a night, a record: A major reason: One of every five hotels is now a shelter, contributing to a shortage of tourist lodging. https://www.nytimes.com/2024/05/25/nyregion/hotels-prices-migrants-nyc.html

Fields, S. (2025, April 28). Four months into congestion pricing, the program is getting more popular – even as the Trump admin attempts to kill it. https://www.marketplace.org/story/2025/04/25/how-congestion-pricing-is-going-4-months-in

Fishman, R. (2007). Revolt of the urbs: Robert Moses and his critics. In H. Ballon & K. T. Jackson (Eds.), *Robert Moses and the modern city: The transformation of New York* (pp. 122–129). W. W. Norton & Company.

Fitch, R. (1993). *The assassination of New York*. Verso.

Flint, A. (2011). *Wrestling with Moses: How Jane Jacobs took on New York's master builder and transformed the American city*. Random House Trade Paperbacks.

Flood, J. (2010). *The fires: How a computer formula, big ideas, and the best of intentions burned down New York City—and determined the future of cities*. Penguin.

Florida, R. (2002). *The rise of the creative class: And how it's transforming work, leisure, community, and everyday life*. Basic Books.

Foderaro, L. W. (1987, May 17). Will it be Loisaida or Alphabet City? Two visions vie in the East Village. *The New York Times*.

Fogelson, R. M. (2013). *The great rent wars: New York, 1917–1929*. Yale University Press.

Foner, N. (2000). *From Ellis Island to JFK: New York's two great waves of immigration*. Yale University Press and Russell Sage Foundation Press.

Foner, N. (2013). Immigrants in New York City in the new millennium. In N. Foner (Ed.), *One out of three: Immigrant New York in the twenty-first century* (pp. 1–34). Columbia University Press.

Foner, N. (2014). Immigration history and the remaking of New York. In N. Foner, J. Rath, J. W. Duyvendak, & R. v. Reekum (Eds.), *New York and Amsterdam: Immigration and the new urban landscape* (pp. 29–51). New York University Press.

Ford, J. (2009). *Hotel on the corner of bitter and sweet*. Ballantine Books.

Ford, L. R. (1994). *Cities and buildings: Skyscrapers, skid rows, and suburbs*. Johns Hopkins University Press.

Forman, A., & Chaban, M. A. V. (2017). *Artists in schools: A creative solution to New York's affordable space crunch*. Center for an Urban Future.

Frank, R. H. (1999). *Luxury fever: Money and happiness in an era of excess*. Princeton University Press.

Frank, R. (2007). *Richistan: A journey through the American wealth boom and the lives of the new rich.* Three Rivers Press.

Freeman, J. B. (2000). *Working class New York: Life and labor since World War II.* The New Press.

Fuchs, E. R. (1992). *Mayors and money: Fiscal policy in New York and Chicago.* The University of Chicago Press.

Fullilove, M. T. (2005). *Root shock: How tearing up city neighborhoods hurts America, and what we can do about it.* One World Ballantine Books.

Galster, G. C. (2012). *Driving Detroit: The quest for respect in the Motor City.* University of Pennsylvania Press.

Garcia, U. J. (2024, January 4). New York City sues bus companies that Texas hired to transport migrants. https://www.texastribune.org/2024/01/04/texas-migrants-new-york-bus-companies-lawsuit/

Garvin, A. (2011). Reflection. In H. Ballon (Ed.), *The greatest grid: The master plan of Manhattan 1811–2011* (p. 139). Museum of the City of New York and Columbia University Press.

Gates, H. L. (1997). Harlem on our minds. *Critical Inquiry, 24*(2), 1–12.

Gladstone, D. L., & Fainstein, S. S. (2013). The New York and Los Angeles economies from boom to crisis. In D. Halle & A. A. Beveridge (Eds.), *New York and Los Angeles: The uncertain future* (pp. 79–102). Oxford University Press.

Glaeser, E. L. (2005, December). *Urban colossus: Why is New York America's largest city?* https://www.newyorkfed.org/medialibrary/media/research/epr/05v11n2/0512glae.pdf

Glaeser, E. (2011). *Triumph of the city: How our greatest invention makes us richer, smarter, greener, healthier, and happier.* Penguin Press.

Glaeser, E., & Cutler, D. (2021). *Survival of the city: Living and thriving in an age of isolation.* Penguin Press.

Glaeser, E., & Gyourko, J. (2018). The economic implications of housing supply. *Journal of Economic Perspectives, 32*(1), 3–30.

Glaeser, E., Gyourko, J., & Saks, R. (2003). *Why is Manhattan so expensive? Regulation and the rise in house prices.* https://www.nber.org/papers/w10124.pdf

Glantz, A. (2019). *Homewreckers: How a gang of Wall Street kingpins, hedge fund magnates, crooked banks, and vulture capitalists suckered millions out of their homes and demolished the American Dream.* Custom House.

Globalization and World Cities Research Network (GaWC; 2024). *The world according to GaWC 2024.* https://www.lboro.ac.uk/gawc/gawcworlds.html

González, J. (2017). *Reclaiming Gotham: Bill de Blasio and the movement to end America's tale of two cities.* The New Press.

Grantsmanship Center, The (n.d.). *Top Giving Foundations: NY.* https://www.tgci.com/funding-sources/NY/top

Gregory, S. (1998). *Black Corona: Race and the politics of place in an urban community.* Princeton University Press.

Greenberg, M. (2008). *Branding New York: How a city in crisis was sold to the world*. Routledge.

Grogan, P. S., & Proscio, T. (2000). *Comeback cities: A blueprint for urban neighborhood revival*. Westview Press.

Gross, J. S., & Savitch, H. V. (2023). *New York*. Agenda Publishing.

Grosser, A. (2024, April 30). Just ten cities are home to nearly a quarter of the world's billionaires. Here's where they choose to live. https://www.forbes.com/sites/annikagrosser/2024/04/26/the-cities-with-the-most-billionaires-2024/

Gurock, J. S. (2019). *Parkchester: A Bronx tale of race and ethnicity*. Washington Mews Books.

Gutfreund, O. D. (2007). Rebuilding New York in the auto age: Robert Moses and his highways. In H. Ballon & K. T. Jackson (Eds.), *Robert Moses and the modern city: The transformation of New York* (pp. 86–93). W. W. Norton & Company.

Gutman, M. (2007). Equipping the public realm: Rethinking Robert Moses and recreation. In H. Ballon & K. T. Jackson (Eds.), *Robert Moses and the modern city: The transformation of New York* (pp. 72–85). W. W. Norton & Company.

Halle, H., & Beveridge, A. A. (2013). New York and Los Angeles: The uncertain future. In D. Halle & A. A. Beveridge (Eds.), *New York and Los Angeles: The uncertain future* (pp. 1–30). Oxford University Press.

Halle, D., Vanstrom, E., Reiff, J., & Nitschke, T. (2013). New York, Los Angeles, and Chicago as depicted in hit movies. In D. Halle & A. A. Beveridge (Eds.), *New York and Los Angeles: The uncertain future* (pp. 484–512). Oxford University Press.

Hamill, P. (2004). *Downtown: My Manhattan*. Back Bay Books.

Hanlon, P. (2017). *A worldly affair: New York, the United Nations, and the story behind their unlikely bond*. Fordham University Press.

Harrington, B. (2016). *Capital without borders: Wealth managers and the one percent*. Harvard University Press.

Harvey, D. (1989). From managerialism to entrepreneurialism: The transformation in urban governance in late capitalism. *Geografiska Annaler. Series B*, 71(1), 3–17.

Hassell, M. v. (1999). *Homesteading in New York City, 1978–1993: The divided heart of Loisaida*. Bergin & Garvey.

Heathcott, J. (2023). *Global Queens: An urban mosaic*. Fordham University Press.

Helmreich, W. B. (2013). *The New York nobody knows: Walking 6 000 miles in the city*. Princeton University Press.

Helmreich, W. B. (2016). *The Brooklyn nobody knows: An urban walking guide*. Princeton University Press.

Helmreich, W. B. (2018). *The Manhattan nobody knows: An urban walking guide*. Princeton University Press.

Helmreich, W. B. (2020). *The Queens nobody knows: An urban walking guide.* Princeton University Press.

Helmreich, W. B. (2023). *The Bronx nobody knows: An urban walking guide.* Princeton University Press.

Highsmith, A. R. (2015). *Demolition means progress: Flint, Michigan, and the fate of the American metropolis.* The University of Chicago Press.

Hilderban, G. (Director, Producer), Vazquez, V. (Director, Producer), Martinez, N. (Producer), & Allen J. (Producer). (2020). *Decade of fire* [Film]. Bayview Entertainment.

Hock, J. (2016). Jane Jacobs. In N. D. Bloom & M. G. Lasner (Eds.), *Affordable housing in New York: The people, the places, and policies that transformed a City* (pp. 207–209). Columbia University Press.

Hodges, G. R. G. (2020). *Taxi! A social history of the New York city cabdriver.* Johns Hopkins University Press.

Holtzman, B. (2016). Urban homesteading. In N. D. Bloom & M. G. Lasner (Eds.), *Affordable housing in New York: The people, the places, and policies that transformed a city* (pp. 258–261). Columbia University Press.

Holtzman, B. (2021). *The long crisis: New York City and the path to neoliberalism.* Oxford University Press.

Hood, C. (2017). *In pursuit of privilege: A history of New York City's upper class and the making of a metropolis.* Columbia University Press.

Howard, E. (2013). *Homeless: Poverty and place in urban America.* University of Pennsylvania Press.

Howe, B. R. (2010). *My Korean deli: Risking it all for a convenience store.* Picador.

Hum, T. (2014). *Making a global immigrant neighborhood: Brooklyn's Sunset Park.* Temple University Press.

Hum, T. (2021). Introduction: Immigrant crossroads. In T. Hum, R. Hayduk, F. Pierre-Louis, & M. Krasner (Eds.), *Immigrant crossroads: Globalization, incorporation, and placemaking in Queens, New York* (pp. 1–23). Temple University Press.

Hyra, D. S. (2008). *The new urban renewal: The economic transformation of Harlem and Bronzeville.* The University of Chicago Press.

Independent Budget Office of the City of New York (n.d.). *About IBO.* https://ibo.nyc.ny.us/aboutibo.html

Jackson, K. T. (2007a). Robert Moses and the rise of New York. In H. Ballon & K. T. Jackson (Eds.), *Robert Moses and the modern city: The transformation of New York* (pp. 67–71). W. W. Norton & Company.

Jackson, K. T. (2007b). Introduction. In C. G. Copquin, *The neighborhoods of Queens* (pp. xxi–xxviii). Yale University Press.

Jaffe, A. (2007). Frank Morales interviewed by Aaron Jaffe in the Odessa coffee shop, Avenue A, Lower East Side. In C. Patterson (Ed.), *Resistance: A radical political and social history of the Lower East Side* (pp. 193–212). Seven Stories Press.

Jennings, C. R. (2018). Urban security in New York City after 9/11: Risk and realities. In S. Opotow & Z. B. Shemtob (Eds.), *New York after 9/11* (pp. 106–127). Fordham University Press.

Johnson, D. A. (1996). *Planning the great metropolis: The 1929 Regional Plan of New York and Its Environs*. Routledge.

Jones, S. H., & Menschel, R. (2011). Preface. In H. Ballon (Ed.), *The greatest grid: The master plan of Manhattan 1811–2011* (p. 9). Museum of the City of New York and Columbia University Press.

Jonnes, J. (2002). *South Bronx rising: The rise, fall, and resurrection of an American city*. Fordham University Press.

Kaiser, C. (2019). *The gay metropolis: The landmark history of gay life in America*. Grove Press.

Kallick, D. D. (2013). Immigration and economic growth in New York City. In N. Foner (Ed.), *One out of three: Immigrant New York in the twenty-first century* (pp. 65–89). Columbia University Press.

Kallick, D. D. (2021). The Queens economy: Where global meets local. In T. Hum, R. Hayduk, F. Pierre-Louis, & M. Krasner (Eds.), *Immigrant crossroads: Globalization, incorporation, and placemaking in Queens, New York* (pp. 47–65). Temple University Press.

Kantor, H. A. (1994). Charles Dyer Norton and the origins of the Regional Plan of New York. In D. Krueckeberg (Ed.), *The American planner: Biographies and recollections* (pp. 163–181). Center for Urban Policy Research.

Kantor, P., Lefèvre, C., Saito, A., Savitch, H. V., & Thornley, A. (2012). *Struggling giants: City–region governance in London, New York, Paris, and Tokyo*. University of Minnesota Press.

Katz, B., & Bradley, J. (2013). *The metropolitan revolution: How cities and metros are fixing our broken politics and fragile economy*. Brookings Institution Press.

Kessner, T. (2003). *Capital city: New York City and the men behind America's rise to economic dominance, 1860–1900*. Simon & Schuster.

Kinder, K. (2016). *DIY Detroit: Making do in a city without services*. University of Minnesota Press.

Kingsley, G. T., Smith, R., & Price, D. (2009). *The impacts of foreclosures on families and communities: A primer*. Urban Institute.

Kirshner, J. A. (2019). *Broke: Hardship and resilience in a city of broken promises*. St. Martin's Press.

Koch, E. I. (1985, January 30). *The State of the City: Housing Initiatives*. Speech.

Koeppel, G. (2015). *City on a grid: How New York became New York*. Da Capo Press.

Kuttner, R. (2021, February 9). *A tale of two developments: Affordable housing or subsidized ultra-luxury? The American Prospect*. https://prospect.org/infrastructure/housing/tale-of-two-developments-affordable-housing-or-subsidized-ultra-luxury/

Lander, B. (2024, January 17). *Spotlight: New York City's rental housing market.* https://comptroller.nyc.gov/reports/spotlight-new-york-citys-rental-housing-market/

Larson, S. (2013). *"Building like Moses with Jacobs in mind": Contemporary planning in New York City.* Temple University Press.

Larson, S. (2017). A High Line for Queens: Celebrating diversity of displacing it? In C. Lindner & B. Rosa (Eds.), *Constructing the High Line: Postindustrial urbanism and the rise of the elevated park* (pp. 169–184). Rutgers University Press.

Lasner, M. G. (2016). Penn Station South. In N. D. Bloom & M. G. Lasner (Eds.), *Affordable housing in New York: The people, the places, and policies that transformed a city* (pp. 170–175). Columbia University Press.

Legiardi-Laura, R. (2007). The soul war for the East Village. In C. Patterson (Ed.), *Resistance: A radical political and social history of the Lower East Side* (pp. 227–234). Seven Stories Press.

Levine, S. (2016). Robert F. Wagner, Jr. In N. D. Bloom & M. G. Lasner (Eds.), *Affordable housing in New York: The people, the places, and policies that transformed a city* (pp. 126–127). Columbia University Press.

Lindner, C. (2017). Retro-walking New York. In C. Lindner & B. Rosa (Eds.), *Constructing the High Line: Postindustrial urbanism and the rise of the elevated park* (pp. 92–105). Rutgers University Press.

Lindner, C., & Rosa, B. (Eds.). (2017). *Constructing the High Line: Postindustrial urbanism and the rise of the elevated park.* Rutgers University Press.

Lobo, A.P., & Salvo, J. J. (2013). A portrait of New York's immigrant mélange. In N. Foner (Ed.), *One out of three: Immigrant New York in the twenty-first century* (pp. 35–89). Columbia University Press.

Loughran, K. (2017). Parks for profit: Public space and inequality in New York City. In C. Lindner & B. Rosa (Eds.), *Constructing the High Line: Postindustrial urbanism and the rise of the elevated park* (pp. 61–91). Rutgers University Press.

Ludwig, B. (2013). Liberians: Struggles for refugee families. In N. Foner (Ed.), *One out of three: Immigrant New York in the twenty-first century* (pp. 200–222). Columbia University Press.

Lynch, L. (n.d.). *Mapping newspaper row: Cartography and the 19th century news landscape.* https://lisallynch.com/mapping-new-york-media/

Macaulay-Lewis, E. (2021). *Antiquity in Gotham: The ancient architecture of New York City.* Fordham University Press.

MacKay, R. B. (Ed.). (2013). *Gardens of Eden: Long Island's early twentieth-century planned communities.* W. W. Norton & Company.

Maffi, M. (1995). *Gateway to the promised land: Ethnic cultures in New York's Lower East Side.* New York University Press.

Mallach, A., & Swanstrom, T. (2023). *The changing American neighborhood: The meaning of place in the twenty-first century.* Cornell University Press.

Manbeck, J. B. (Ed.). (2004). *The neighborhoods of Brooklyn*. Yale University Press.

Manshel, A. M. (2020). *Learning from Bryant Park: Revitalizing cities, towns, and public spaces*. Rutgers University Press.

Marwell, N. (2007). *Bargaining for Brooklyn: Community organizations in the entrepreneurial city*. The University of Chicago Press.

Matsumoto, N. (2018). *Beyond the city and the bridge: East Asian immigration in a New Jersey suburb*. Rutgers University Press.

Maurrasse, D. J. (2006). *Listening to Harlem: Gentrification, community, and business*. Routledge.

McCormick, L. (2021). The restructuring of manufacturing in Queens and its impact on immigrant workers. In T. Hum, R. Hayduk, F. Pierre-Louis, & M. A. Krasner (Eds.), *Immigrant crossroads: Globalization, incorporation, and placemaking in Queens, New York* (pp. 66–94). Temple University Press.

McEvilley, T. (2007). Twenty-one years on the Lower East Side. In C. Patterson (Ed.), *Resistance: A radical political and social history of the Lower East Side* (pp. 37–39). Seven Stories Press.

McGeehan, P. (2016, March 8). Record number of tourists visited New York City in 2015, and more are expected this year. *The New York Times*.

McPhee, J. (1983). *Suspect terrain*. Farrar, Straus and Giroux.

Medoff, P., & Sklar, H. (1994). *Streets of hope: The fall and rise of an urban neighborhood*. South End Press.

Mele, C. (2000). *Selling the Lower East Side: Culture, real estate, and resistance in New York City*. University of Minnesota Press.

Mele, C. (2007). Making art and policing streets. In C. Patterson (Ed.), *Resistance: A radical political and social history of the Lower East Side* (pp. 40–47). Seven Stories Press

Melosi, M. V. (2020). *Fresh kills: A history of consuming and discarding in New York City*. Columbia University Press.

Mensch, B. G. (2018). *In the shadow of genius: The Brooklyn Bridge and its creators*. Fordham University Press.

Metropolitan Transit Authority (n.d.). *Tickets, tokens, and MetroCards*. https://new.mta.info/fares

Milambiling, J. (2023). *Skyscraper settlement: The many lives of Christodora House*. New Village Press.

Min, P. G. (2013). Koreans: Changes in New York in the twenty-first century. In N. Foner (Ed.), *One out of three: Immigrant New York in the twenty-first century* (pp. 148–175). Columbia University Press.

Mogilevich, M. (2016). John Lindsay. In N. D. Bloom & M. G. Lasner (Eds.), *Affordable housing in New York: The people, the places, and policies that transformed a city* (pp. 213–215). Columbia University Press.

Mollenkopf, J. (1992). *A Phoenix in the ashes: The rise and fall of the Koch coalition in New York City politics*. Princeton University Press.

Mollenkopf, J. (Ed.) (2005). *Contentious city: The politics of recovery in New York City*. Russell Sage Foundation.

Mollenkopf, J., & Sonenshein, R. J. (2013). New York City and Los Angeles: Government and political influence. In D. Halle & A. A. Beveridge (Eds.), *New York and Los Angeles: The uncertain future* (pp. 137–153). Oxford University Press.

Molotch, H. (1976). The city as a growth machine: Toward a political economy of place. *American Journal of Sociology, 82*(2), 309–332.

Morris, E. (2015). *Wall Streeters: The creators and corruptors of American finance.* Columbia Business School Publishing.

Moss, J. (2017). *Vanishing New York: How a great city lost its soul.* Dey St.

Moss, M. L. (2005). The redevelopment of Lower Manhattan: The role of the city. In J. Mollenkopf (Ed.), *Contentious city: The politics of recovery in New York City* (pp. 95–111). Russell Sage Foundation.

Nahmias, N., & Cattan, N. (2024, November 22). NYC gets historic push for 80,000 homes with $5 billion pledge: "City of Yes" rezoning plan is approved by key council Panel: Aim is to address city's worst housing shortage in 5 decades. https://www.bloomberg.com/news/articles/2024-11-22/nyc-gets-historic-push-for-80-000-homes-with-5-billion-pledge?utm_content=citylab&utm_source=facebook&utm_campaign=socialflow-organic&utm_medium=social&fbclid=IwY2xjawGus_lleHRu-A2FlbQIxMQABHa82f51YbxcMMJlCNetR8MD3lHBIh0uL4CHB-pqVPUmXsvlNkASvNYRNFYw_aem__M7knKBz91Hi_0gdCUXQ4A

National Housing Conference. (n.d.). *About NHC.* https://nhc.org/

National Low Income Housing Coalition. (2020). *Out of reach.* https://reports.nlihc.org/oor

Nave, P. (n.d.). 15 cities with the most Fortune 500 headquarters. https://axiomalpha.com/15-cities-with-the-most-fortune-500-headquarters-2022/

Nevlus, J. (2018, June 27). *The elevated era: The "El" was the city's first real attempt to reclaim the street.* https://ny.curbed.com/2018/6/27/17507424/new-york-city-elevated-train-history-transportation

New York City Economic Development Corporation (n.d.a). *Doing business in New York City.* https://edc.nyc/doing-business-new-york-city

New York City Economic Development Corporation (n.d.b). *Industrial and manufacturing.* https://edc.nyc/industry/industrial-and-manufacturing

New York City Housing Authority (2022). *NYCHA 2022 fact sheet.* https://www.nyc.gov/assets/nycha/downloads/pdf/NYCHA_Fact_Sheet_2022.pdf

New York City Housing Development Corporation. (n.d.a). *About us.* http://www.nychdc.com

New York City Housing Development Corporation. (n.d.b). *HDC: A brief history.* http://www.nychdc.com/HDC_%20A_%20Brief_History#:~:text=In%201971%2C%20the%20New%20York,from%20the%20City's%20capital%20budget.

New York City Housing Preservation and Development (n.d.). *The housing plan: Your home NYC.* https://www1.nyc.gov/site/housing/index.page

New York City Industrial Development Agency (n.d.). *Tax benefits for your business*. https://edc.nyc/nycida

New York City Parks (n.d.). *Robert Moses and the Modern Park System (1929–1965)*. https://www.nycgovparks.org/about/history/timeline/robert-moses-modern-parks#:~:text=As%20chairmen%20of%20the%20New,natural%20areas%20in%20the%20city.

New York City Rent Guidelines Board. (2024). *Housing NYC: Rents, markets, and trends 2024*. https://rentguidelinesboard.cityofnewyork.us/wp-content/uploads/2024/10/2024-HNYC-Book.pdf

NYC & Company (n.d.a). *Our mission*. https://business.nycgo.com/about-us/who-we-are/

NYC & Company (n.d.b). *NYC & Company annual report 2019–2020*. https://indd.adobe.com/view/a614092f-2162-4a39-97c3-f4d67b0cbe0b

NYC Urbanism (n.d.). *Roosevelt Island*. https://www.nycurbanism.com/brutalnyc/2017/2/15/eastwood

NYU Furman Center (n.d.). *Directory of NYC housing programs*. https://furmancenter.org/coredata/directory/all

Oberlander, H. P., & Newbrun, E. (1999). *Houser: The life and work of Catherine Bauer*. University of British Columbia Press.

Ocejo, R. E. (2014). *Upscaling downtown: From Bowery saloons to cocktail bars in New York City*. Princeton University Press.

Office of the New York State Comptroller. (2023). *NYC's shifting population: The latest statistics*. https://www.osc.ny.gov/files/reports/osdc/pdf/report-15-2024.pdf?utm_medium=email&utm_source=govdelivery

Office of the Texas Governor (2024, January 12). Texas transports over 100,000 migrants to sanctuary cities. https://gov.texas.gov/news/post/texas-transports-over-100000-migrants-to-sanctuary-cities

Onishi, N. (1994, March 13). Police announce crackdown on quality-of-life offenses. *The New York Times*.

Order Sons and Daughters of Italy in America (n.d.). *History*. https://osdia.org/about/history/

Osman, S. (2011). *The invention of brownstone Brooklyn: Gentrification and the search for authenticity in postwar New York*. Oxford University Press.

Osofsky, G. (1996). *Harlem: The making of a ghetto: [Black] New York, 1890–1930*. Ivan R. Dee.

Parker, D. (1928, January). My home town. *McCall's*, *55*(4), 6.

Partnership for New York City (n.d.). *About*. https://pfnyc.org/about/#

Phillips-Fein, K. (2011, October 19). In bleak '70s, salvo of protest. *The New York Times*.

Phillips-Fein, K. (2017). *Fear city: New York's fiscal crisis and the rise of austerity politics*. Picador.

Plotch, P. M. (2020). *Last subway: The long wait for the next train in New York City*. Three Hills.

Plunz, R. (2016). *A history of housing in New York City*. Columbia University Press.

Plunz, R., & Abu-Lughod, J. (1994). The tenement as a built form. In J. Abu-Lughod, *From urban village to East Village: The battle for New York's Lower East Side* (pp. 63–79). Blackwell.

Podemski, M. (2024). *A paradise of small houses: The evolution, devolution, and potential rebirth of urban housing*. Beacon Press.

Powell, M. (2009, October 25). Another look at the Dinkins administration, and not by Giuliani. *The New York Times*.

Pritchett, W. (2002). *Brownsville, Brooklyn: Blacks, Jews, and the changing face of the ghetto*. The University of Chicago Press.

Quinn, P. (2022). *Cross Bronx: A writing life*. Fordham University Press.

Raskin, J. B. (2014). *The routes not taken: A trip through New York City's unbuilt subway system*. Fordham University Press.

Rath, J., Foner, N., Duyvendak, J. W., & Reekum, R. v. (2014). Introduction: New York and Amsterdam: Immigration and the new urban landscape. In N. Foner, J. Rath, J. W. Duyvendak, & R. v. Reekum (Eds.), *New York and Amsterdam: Immigration and the new urban landscape* (pp. 1–21). New York University Press.

Regional Plan Association (n.d.). *Regional plan of New York and its environs*. Regional Plan Association.

Regional Plan Association. (2018). *NYCHA's crisis: A matter for all New Yorkers*. https://s3.us-east-1.amazonaws.com/rpa-org/pdfs/RPA-NYCHAs_Crisis_2018_12_18.pdf

Revell, K. D. (2003). *Building Gotham: Civic culture and policy in New York City, 1898–1938*. Johns Hopkins University Press.

Roberts, S. (2006, December 28). Infamous "drop dead" was never said by Ford. *The New York Times*.

Rosa, B., & Lindner, C. (2017). Introduction: From elevated railway to urban park. In C. Lindner & B. Rosa (Eds.), *Constructing the High Line: Postindustrial urbanism and the rise of the elevated park* (pp. 1–20). Rutgers University Press.

Rose-Redwood, R. (2011). Numbering and naming Manhattan's streets. In H. Ballon (Ed.), *The greatest grid: The master plan of Manhattan 1811–2011* (p. 95). Museum of the City of New York and Columbia University Press.

Rosenberg, E. (2014, January 16). *How NYC's decade of rezoning changed the City of Industry*. Curbed.

Saegert, S., & Winkel, G. (1998). Social capital and the revitalization of New York City's distressed inner-city housing. *Housing Policy Debate*, *9*(1), 17–60.

Sagalyn, L. B. (2005). The politics of planning the world's most visible urban redevelopment project. In J. Mollenkopf (Ed.), *Contentious city: The politics of recovery in New York City* (pp. 23–72). Russell Sage Foundation.

Sagalyn, L. B. (2016). *Power at Ground Zero: Politics, money, and the remaking of Lower Manhattan*. Oxford University Press.

Salins, P. D. (1999). Reviving New York City's housing market. In M. H. Schill (Ed.), *Housing and community development in New York City: Facing the future* (pp. 53–71). State University of New York Press.

Salvo, J. J., & Lobo, A. P. (2021). Queens neighborhoods: From European strongholds to global microcosms. In T. Hum, R. Hayduk, F. Pierre-Louis, & M. Krasner (Eds.), *Immigrant crossroads: Globalization, incorporation, and placemaking in Queens, New York* (pp. 27–46). Temple University Press.

Sambeck, B. V. (2025, April 21). *Which industries are recession-proof? Careers that weather economic downturn*. https://online.usc.edu/news/recession-proof-industries-careers-economic-downturn/

Sanders, H. T. (2014). *Convention center follies: Politics, power, and public investment in American cities*. University of Pennsylvania Press.

Sanders, J. (2002, September 1). Ideas and trends: Thinking big; in New York, seeking a grand vision of public works. *The New York Times*.

Sassen, S. (2001). *The global city: New York, London, Tokyo*. Princeton University Press.

Sawadogo, B. (2022). *Africans in Harlem: An untold New York story*. Fordham University Press.

Sawhill, I. (2018). *The forgotten Americans: An economic agenda for a divided nation*. Yale University Press.

Schill, M. H., Ellen, I. G., Schwartz, A. E., & Voicu, I. (2002). Revitalizing inner-city neighborhoods: New York's ten-year plan. *Housing Policy Debate, 13*(3), 529–566.

Schill, M. H., & Scafidi, B. P. (1999). Housing conditions and problems in New York City. In M. H. Schill (Ed.), *Housing and community development in New York City: Facing the future* (pp. 11–52). State University of New York Press.

Schlichting, K. M. (2019). *New York recentered: Building the metropolis from the shore*. The University of Chicago Press.

Schwab, K. (2025, January 8). New York City's congestion pricing will add costs for businesses, but there are workarounds. https://www.marketplace.org/story/2025/01/08/new-york-city-congestion-pricing-businesses-delivery-shipping-logistics

Schwartz, A. (2019). New York City's affordable housing plans and the limits of local initiative. *Cityscape, 21*(3), 355–388.

Schwartz, J. (2007). Robert Moses and city planning. In H. Ballon & K. T. Jackson (Eds.), *Robert Moses and the modern city: The transformation of New York* (pp. 130–133). W. W. Norton & Company.

Seidlein, L. v., Alabaster, G., Deen, J., & Knudsen, J. (2021). Crowding has consequences: Prevention and management of COVID-19 in informal urban settlements. *Building and Environment, 188*, 107472.

Sharman, R. L. (2006). *The tenants of East Harlem*. University of California Press.
Shemtob, Z. B., Sweeney, P., & Opotow, S. (2018). Conflict and change: New York City's rebirth after 9/11. In S. Opotow & Z. B. Shemtob (Eds.), *New York after 9/11* (pp. 14–40). Fordham University Press.
Shepard, B. H., & Noonan, M. J. (2018). *Brooklyn tides: The fall and rise of a global borough*. Transcript.
Shorto, R. (2025). *Taking Manhattan: The extraordinary events that created New York and shaped America*. W. W. Norton & Company.
Smart, A. (2017). Loving the High Line: Infrastructure, architecture, and the politics of space in the mediated city. In C. Lindner & B. Rosa (Eds.), *Constructing the High Line: Postindustrial urbanism and the rise of the elevated park* (pp. 41–58). Rutgers University Press.
Smithsonian Institution (n.d.). *German Society of the City of New York*. https://americanhistory.si.edu/steinwaydiary/annotations/?id=852
Soffer, J. (2010). *Ed Koch and the rebuilding of New York City*. Columbia University Press.
Soffer, J. (2016). The Koch housing plan In N. D. Bloom & M. G. Lasner (Eds.), *Affordable housing in New York: The people, the places, and policies that transformed a city* (pp. 273–276). Columbia University Press.
Sorkin, M. (2009). *Twenty minutes in Manhattan*. North Point Press.
Spady, M. (2020). *The neighborhood Manhattan forgot: Audubon Park and the families who shaped it*. Fordham University Press.
Spicer, J. S., Stephens, L., & Kramer, A. (2024). Oranges are not the only fruit: The publicly owned variety of Community Land Trusts. *Journal of Planning Education and Research, 44*(3), 1775–1790.
Steinberg, T. (2014). *Gotham unbound: The ecological history of greater New York*. Simon & Schuster.
Stern, E., & Yager, J. (2016). *Selling the debt: Properties affected by the sale of New York City tax liens*. https://furmancenter.org/files/NYU_Furman_Center_SellingtheDebt_28JULY2016.pdf
Stiman, M. (2024). *Privileging place: How second homeowners transform communities and themselves*. Princeton University Press.
StreetEasy (2018, January 11). *Those confusing Queens streets, explained*. https://streeteasy.com/blog/queens-addresses-hyphenated-confusing-street-names/
Sweeting, G., & Dinneen, A. (2013). New York and Los Angeles: Taxes, budgets, and managing the financial crisis. In D. Halle & A. A. Beveridge (Eds.), *New York and Los Angeles: The uncertain future* (pp. 193–216). Oxford University Press.
Taborn, K. (2018). *Walking Harlem: The ultimate guide to the cultural capital of Black America*. Rutgers University Press.

Terry, D. (1990, May 17). Dinkins expands housing plan to assist the poor. *The New York Times*.

Thabit, W. (2003). *How East New York became a ghetto*. New York University Press.

Tippins, S. (2013). *Inside the dream palace: The life and times of New York's legendary Chelsea Hotel*. Houghton Mifflin Harcourt.

Traub, J. (2011). Reflection. In H. Ballon (Ed.), *The greatest grid: The master plan of Manhattan 1811–2011* (p. 85). Museum of the City of New York and Columbia University Press.

U.S. Bureau of the Census. (n.d.a). *Decennial Census of Population and Housing*. https://www.census.gov/programs-surveys/decennial-census.html#:~:text=The%20U.S.%20census%20counts%20each,of%20Representatives%20among%20the%20states.

U.S. Bureau of the Census (n.d.b). Quick facts: New York City, New York. https://www.census.gov/quickfacts/fact/table/newyorkcitynewyork/PST045224

U.S. Bureau of the Census (n.d.c). Metropolitan and micropolitan statistical areas population totals: 2020–2023. https://www.census.gov/data/tables/time-series/demo/popest/2020s-total-metro-and-micro-statistical-areas.html#v2023

U.S. Bureau of Labor Statistics (n.d.). *Quarterly Census of Employment and Wages*. https://data.bls.gov/cew/apps/table_maker/v4/table_maker.htm#type=5&year=2024&qtr=2&own=3&area=36061&supp=0

U.S. Department of Housing and Urban Development (n.d.). *Affordable housing*. https://www.hud.gov/DrivingAffordableHousing/affordablehousing

Van Ryzin, G., & Genn, A. (1999). Neighborhood change and the city of New York's ten-year housing plan. *Housing Policy Debate, 10*(4), 799–838.

Venkatesh, S. (2013). *Floating city: A rogue sociologist lost and found in New York's underground economy*. Penguin Books.

Vergara, C. J. (2013). *Harlem: The unmaking of a ghetto*. The University of Chicago Press.

Vickerman, M. (2013). Jamaicans: Balancing race and ethnicity. In N. Foner (Ed.), *One out of three: Immigrant New York in the twenty-first century* (pp. 176–199). Columbia University Press.

Vitale, A. S. (2008). *City of disorder: How the quality of life campaign transformed New York politics*. New York University Press.

von Hoffman, A. (2003). *House by house, block by block: The rebirth of America's urban neighborhoods*. Oxford University Press.

Wallace, M. (2017). *Greater Gotham: A history of New York City from 1898 to 1919*. Oxford University Press.

Walters, S. J. K. (2014). *Boom towns: Restoring the urban American Dream*. Stanford University Press.

Wilkerson, I. (2010). *The warmth of other suns: The epic story of America's great migration*. Vintage Books.

Willis, M., Austensen, M., Moriarty, S., Rosoff, S., & Sanders, T. (2016). *Report on homeownership and opportunity in New York City*. https://community-wealth.org/sites/clone.community-wealth.org/files/downloads/paper-willis-et-al.pdf

Wirka, S. M. (1996). The city social movement: Progressive women reformers and early social planning. In M. C. Sies & C. Silver (Eds.), *Planning the twentieth-century American city* (pp. 55–75). Johns Hopkins University Press.

Wolf-Powers, L. (2014). New York City's community-based housing movement: Achievements and prospects. In N. Gallent & D. Ciaffi (Eds.), *Community action and planning: Contexts, drivers and outcomes* (pp. 217–235). Policy Press.

Woodsworth, M. (2016). *Battle for Bed-Stuy: The long war on poverty in New York City*. Harvard University Press.

Zelasnic, L. (2007). Timetable. In C. Patterson (Ed.), *Resistance: A radical political and social history of the Lower East Side* (pp. 237–251). Seven Stories Press.

Zhou, M. (2013). Chinese: Diverse origins and destinies. In N. Foner (Ed.), *One out of three: Immigrant New York in the twenty-first century* (pp. 120–147). Columbia University Press.

Ziegler-McPherson, C. A. (2022). *The great disappearing act: Germans in New York City, 1880–1930*. Rutgers University Press.

Zipp, S. (2010). *Manhattan projects: The rise and fall of urban renewal in Cold War New York*. Oxford University Press.

Zukin, S. (1989). *Loft living: Culture and capital in urban change*. Rutgers University Press.

Zukin, S. (1991). *Landscapes of power: From Detroit to Disney World*. University of California Press.

Zukin, S. (1995). *The cultures of cities*. Blackwell.

Zukin, S. (2010). *Naked city: The death and life of authentic urban places*. Oxford University Press.

Zukin, S., Kasinitz, P., & Chen, X. (2016). Spaces of everyday diversity: The patchwork ecosystem of local shopping streets. In S. Zukin, P. Kasinitz, & X. Chen (Eds.), *Global cities, local streets: Everyday diversity from New York to Shanghai* (pp. 1–28). Routledge.

INDEX

125th Street (Dr. Martin Luther King Jr. Boulevard) 14, 73, 92, 94

abatements (property tax) 50, 73–74
Abbott, Greg 28
Adam Clayton Powell Jr. Boulevard *see* Seventh Avenue (Adam Clayton Powell Jr. Boulevard)
Adams, Mayor Eric 28; *City of Yes for Housing Opportunity* (COYFHA) 100–101
affordable housing *see* housing
African Methodist Episcopal Zion Church 15
African Society for Mutual Relief 15
airfields 66
airports 64, 66, 95
Alfred, Helen 70
Algonquin tribe 10
Alliance for Downtown New York 72, 76
"Alphabet City" 91
Amalgamated Clothing Workers Union of America (ACWU) 71
American Company of Booksellers 21
American Sugar Refining Company 18
Andrew W. Mellon Foundation 35
Apollo, Harlem 92
area (land area of NYC) 86
Armstrong, Louis 92, 96
arson 26, 43, 44, 58
art collections 35
art galleries 35, 45, 52
artists 24, 35–36, 45, 91
art movements 35–36, 45
art (public) 35
artworks: The Gates (Christo and Jeanne-Claude) 76
Asian population 26, 30–31, 56, 96
Association for a Better New York (ABNY) 72, 74
Association for Improving the Conditions of the Poor (AICP) 69
Atlantic Ocean 5, 8, 9
Atlantic seaboard location 5, 10, 66, 84
Audubon Ballroom, Harlem 92
austerity measures 42–44, 45, 51
avenues (north–south) 13–14, 15

Bangladesh (immigrants from) 31, 97
banking: fiscal crises 37, 40; foreign banks 38; funding for Regional Plan Association (RPA) 65, 86; knowledge-based economy 24

Barr, J. M. 49–50
baseball 88, 95
Battery Park City 76, 92
Bauer, Catherine 70
Bayonne Bridge, New Jersey 67
beat writers 35–36
bedrock (Manhattan schist) 49
Beijing, China 12
Bergdorf Goodman [department store] 20
Berkowitz, David 44
Bicentennial 75
Big Apple marketing campaign 74–75
billionaires 34
Birdland Jazz Club 91
Black/African American population 26, 53; access to entertainment venues 93; Brooklyn 88; displacement 15; Great Migration 93; Harlem 92, 93–94; housing 56; Lower East Side 90; Queens 96
"Black Monday" 36
blackouts (July 1977) 44
Black-owned establishments 93
Blackwell's Island *see* Roosevelt Island
de Blasio, Mayor Bill 76; *Housing New York 2.0* (2017) 59, 60–61; *Housing New York: A Five-Borough Ten-year Housing Plan* (2014) 59, 60; *YOUR Home NYC* (2020) 59
blockbusting 88
blocks 13, 16
Bloomberg, Mayor Michael 3, 76; *Bloomberg Plan* (2002) 59, 60; *New Housing Marketplace Plan* (NHMP) (2003) 59, 60; *PlanNYC 2030* (2007) 59
Bloomberg Plan (2002) 59, 60
blue-collar manufacturing 16–17, 84
Board of Estimate (BoE) 80

bodegas 91
bonds 39, 40–42, 67, 73, 74, 81
book fairs 21
boosterism 36, 69, 71, 77
Borough Presidents 62
boroughs 5, 7, 86, 95
Boston 8, 12, 87
boulevards 13
boycotts (of Korean stores) 29
brewing industry (Brooklyn) 87
bridges 66, 67–68, 80, 87; *see also individual bridges*
broadcasting *see* radio stations; television stations
Broadway 13, 24, 52
Bronx (Bronx County) 13, 94; fires/arson 43, 95; (immigrant) population 32, 94–95; impact of austerity measures 43; Kingsbridge Heights/Moshulu 48; South Bronx 43, 94, 95; urbanization 87
Brooklyn: brewing industry 87; bridges 68, 87; Bulk Flour Center 18; Ebbets Field 88; ethnic/racial diversity 32, 88, 89; famous establishments 88; gentrification 88; gridiron (street grid) 13; housing 86–87, 88; impact of austerity measures 43; manufacturing industry 20, 87; neighborhoods 87; population 25, 87; port facilities 66; Prospect Park 52; sugar production 18; urbanization 87; *see also* Williamsburg, Brooklyn
Brooklyn Bridge 68, 87
Brooklyn Bridge Park 52
Brooklyn Dodgers 88
Brooklyn Heights 24
Brooklyn-Manhattan Transit Corporation (BMT) transit line 68

Brooklyn Rapid Transit Company (BRT) 68
brownstones 87, 88
Bryant Park Corporation, Manhattan 73
Bryant Park, Midtown 52
budget (NYC) 39, 41–42, 62, 63
building materials (cost of) 50
Building Zone Resolution (1916) 86
Bulk Flour Center, Brooklyn 18
business improvement districts (BID) 73, 76
business leaders *see* Partnership for New York City
business ownership 31
bus routes 97
bus terminals 66

canal system 8
capital (concentration of) 34, 36, 84
capitalism 3
"capital of culture" (NYC as) 3, 35, 84
capital (state) 16
Caribbean immigrants/population 31, 88
Carnegie Hall 52, 91
carnicerias 91
Caro, Robert: *The Power Broker: Robert Moses and the Fall of New York* 84
car ownership 79
Carter, President Jimmy 41
casitas 91
Castle Garden Emigrant Landing Depot 29
CBS (Columbia Broadcasting Company) 23
Central Business District (Manhattan) 64
Central European immigrants 90
Central Harlem *see* Harlem
Central Park 15, 24, 52; The Gates (Christo and Jeanne-Claude) 76
Chelsea 24, 92
Chicago 25, 81, 86, 87
China (garment imports) 20
Chinatown (Manhattan) 20, 24, 48, 49, 50, 89, 92
Chinese Exclusion Act (1882) 27
Chinese immigrants 29, 30, 31, 89
cities (role/rankings) 33–34
City Council 51
City Hall 12, 21, 68
City of Yes for Housing Opportunity (COYFHA) 100–101
City Planning Commission (CPC) 51, 63, 79, 80
City University of New York (CUNY) 42
civic associations 69, 74, 78
civic-mindedness (civicism) 3
civil enforcement 46
civil rights activists 92
Civil Service Commission 78
civil unrest (Harlem) 93
climate change (impact of) 99–100
coastal storm (surges) 99
cocaine use 45
colleges (municipal) 39
Colombian immigrants 31
Columbia Broadcasting Company (CBS) *see* CBS (Columbia Broadcasting Company)
Columbia University 16
Columbus Circle 89, 92
Common Council 12
Community Boards (CB) 51, 62
Community Parks Initiative 51
comptroller 62, 80
condominiums 55, 57
conflicts (residents vs. immigrants) 29
congestion pricing 64

congestion (traffic) 15; traffic 50
construction industry: construction costs 50; geological features 49; immigrant workforce 29, 89; WPA-supported jobs 35
container shipping 66, 67
Convention and Visitors Bureau (CVB) 74, 76, 77
Co-op City (Bronx) 70, 95
cooperative housing units 55, 57, 70, 95
Cooper Square Committee 83
Corporation Counsel 80
corporations (major/global) 38, 41, 43, 65, 71
corruption (land purchases) 84
Cosell, Howard 95
Cotton Club, Harlem 92
Cotton Triangle 18–19
counties (MSA) 5
COVID-19 pandemic 26, 55, 56, 100
crack epidemic 45
creative individuals 3, 101
creative industries 24, 35–36
crime 44, 45–46, 91; *see also* New York City Police Department (NYPD)
cross streets (east-west) 13
Croton Aqueduct 8
crowding (housing) 55–56, 57
cultural affairs (funding for) 51
cultural attractions 35, 52, 78
culture (capital of) 3, 35, 84
customs duties 8

dancing/dancers 92
David, Joshua 52
debt (outstanding) 39
Delaware tribe *see* Algonquin tribe
Democratic National Convention (1976) 75
demographic resilience 100

demographics 25–28, 30
Department of Buildings 80
Department of City Planning (DCP) 63
Department of Housing Preservation and Development (HPD) 59
Department of Parks 79
Department of Parks and Recreation 51
Department of Sanitation 42
department stores 20
Deputy Mayor of Housing and Economic Development 63
deputy mayors 62–63
destination marketing organization (DMO) 76
development organizations 71–74
DeWitt, Simeon [New York State Surveyor General] 12
Diller, Scofidio + Renfro 52
Dillon's Rule 63
Dinkins, Mayor Dave 45
disease (overcrowded housing) 56
displacement (of residents) 82, 83, 84; for expressways 80–81; following Plan of 1811 15; "root shock" 82; San Juan Hill neighborhood 78
district attorneys 62
diversity (of NYC) 3, 26, 30–31, 84, 93; *see also* immigration
Division of Alternative Management Program (DAMP) 59
Dominican immigrants 30–31, 97
Domino Sugar Refinery, Williamsburg 18
Downtown-Lower Manhattan Association (DLMA) 76
downtown Manhattan *see* Manhattan

Dr. Martin Luther King Jr. Boulevard *see* 125th Street (Dr. Martin Luther King Jr. Boulevard)
drugs 45, 91
Durst Organization 34–35
Dutch immigrants 30
Dutch West India Company (WIC) 11

Eastern European immigrants 30, 32, 90
East Harlem *see* Harlem
East River 8, 13, 49, 68, 89; ferries 68; man-made waterfalls (Olafur Eliasson) 76; manufacturing 18; tunnels 95
East River Tunnels 95
East Village, Manhattan 92
east-west cross streets 13
Ebbets Field, Brooklyn 88
economic resilience 100
economy 2–3, 8, 36; austerity measures 42–44, 45, 51; "Black Monday" 36; budget shortfalls 39; challenges 37–39; creative industries 35–36; development of 16–17, 84; entrepreneurial policies 36–37; FIRE sector 17, 36; fiscal crises 37, 39–45, 84; Fortune 500 companies 34, 38; free market 11; high-net-worth individuals 34, 53; manufacturing sector 16–17, 23, 29, 87; municipal function expenditures 40; outstanding debt 39; over-optimistic forecasting 39; per capita common function debt 39–40; recessions 36, 100; recovery 45; service sector employment 17, 23, 37; *see also* industry
Ecuador (immigrants from) 31, 97

education: expansion of higher education 78, 80; of immigrants 31, 90
"El Barrio" *see* Harlem
elevated transit line 68
Eliasson, Olafur 76
Elizabeth Marine Terminal, Elizabeth, NJ 66
Ellis Island 29
Emergency Financial Control Board (EFCB) 41
employment: business ownership 31; creative industries 36; decrease (austerity measures) 42; ethnic divisions 31; garment industry 19–20, 29, 90; government sector 17; immigrant workforce 29–31, 89, 90; manufacturing 17, 23, 29, 37, 38; printing and publishing 21–22; public sector 38; service sector 17, 23, 37; WPA-supported jobs 35; *see also* location quotients (LQ)
enclaves *see* immigrant neighborhoods
energy costs 50
English immigrants 30
entertainment venues 23, 73, 93
Erie Canal Commission 8
Esquire magazine 21
ethnic diversity (NYC) 26
ethnic neighborhoods *see* immigrant neighborhoods
exceptionalism 69–71, 84
expatriates 34
expressways 80–81
extreme weather 99

factories 94; Brooklyn 18, 87; immigrant workforce 29, 89
Fannie Mae (1938) 58
fashion industry 19–20, 24
Federal Aid Highway Act (1956) 58

Federal Deposit Insurance Corporation (FDIC) (1933) 58
federal function (of NYC) 16
Federal Home Loan Bank Act (1932) 58
federal loans 40, 41
feminist movement 36
ferries 68
Fifth Avenue 24, 50
film and television industry 22
film industry 75–76, 77
Film Production Tax Credit Program 22
finance, insurance, and real estate (FIRE) sector 17, 24, 36
Financial Control Board (FCB) 41–42
Financial District 24, 92
firefighters 42, 43
fires (Bronx) 43, 95
FIRE sector (finance, insurance, and real estate) *see* finance, insurance, and real estate (FIRE) sector
First Deputy Mayor 62
fiscal autonomy 40–41
fiscal crises 37, 39–45, 84
Fitzgerald, Ella 92, 96
flexible deployment 46
Flushing Meadows, Queens (World's Fair) 77, 79, 80
Flushing, Queens 29
Ford Foundation 35, 65
Ford, President 40
foreclosure auctions 58
Fort Green 24
Fortune 500 companies 34, 38
foundations 35, 65, 78
Fourth Regional Plan (2017) 65
Franklin Theater, Harlem 92
Fresh Kills Park 97
Friends of the High Line (FHL) group 52
Fuchs, E. R. 40

gang crime 91
Garment District 19, 20
garment industry 16–17, 18–20, 29, 71, 90
gay movement 36
gentrification: Brooklyn 88; Harlem 93–94; Lower East Side 91; Queens 97
geographical features 49
geological features 49
George Washington Bridge 66–67
German immigrants 29–30, 89
German Society of the City of New York 29
Giuliani, Mayor Rudolph 4, 45
Glaser, Milton 75
global corporations 71
Globalization and World Cities Research Network (GaWC) 33
Goethals Bridge 66
Goldin, Frances 83
goods: imported 8–9; transportation 8–9, 37, 67–68; *see also* canal system: shipping services (scheduled)
Gould, Jay 35
government (New York City) 62–64; Civil Services Commission 78; legislative process 63; powers and rights 63; relationship with state government 63–64
government sector employment 17
Gramercy 50, 92
Grand Central Terminal 16, 92
Great Depression 27, 71, 93
Great Migration 53, 93
Great Recession 56, 100
Greenberg, M.: *Branding New York: How a City in Crisis Was Sold to the World* 77
greenhouse gas emissions 99
Greenpoint, Brooklyn 24, 87

Greenwich Village 12, 35, 49, 50, 89, 92
gridiron (street grid) 13, 15
grocery stores 30, 31, 91
gross national product (GNP) 3
Guyana (immigrants from) 31, 97

Hammond, Robert 52
Harlem 92; 125th Street (Dr. Martin Luther King Boulevard) 14, 73, 92; avenue names 14; Black/African American population 92, 93–94; Central Harlem 48, 93; civil unrest 93; East Harlem (Spanish Harlem/ El Barrio) 89; fire services 43; gentrification 93–94; Great Depression 93; nightlife 92; population 48, 93; racial/ethnic diversity 93–94; transport links 68
Harlem Promenade 52
(New) Harlem Renaissance 92
Harlem Repertory Theatre 92
Harper's Monthly 3
Hart-Cellar Act (1965) *see* Immigration and Nationality (Hart–Cellar) Act (1965)
Haussmann, Baron 78
healthcare services 39, 42
healthcare workers 31
Helmreich, William 2, 95
Henry, O. 1
Henry Street Settlement 70
heroin epidemic 45
higher education (land use) 78
High Line, Manhattan 52
high-net-worth individuals (HNWIs) 34, 53
high-rise housing 81
Hispanic/Latino population 26, 56; Harlem 93; Lower East Side 91; Queens 96

Hoboken, New Jersey 66
Holland Tunnel 66–67
homeless persons 46, 82
homeownership rates 54–55, 57
Home Owners' Loan Corporation (HOLC) (1933) 58
"home rule" 63
horizontal expansion (Manhattan) 13
hospitals 16, 39
household incomes/wealth 53, 55
households (number/size) 47
housing: affordability 43, 44, 47, 48–49, 52–58, 60–61, 100–101; blockbusting 88; condominiums 55, 57; cooperative housing units 55, 57, 70, 95; crowding 55–56, 57; high-rise 81; low vs. high-cost 48–49, 60–61; luxury 37; municipal 39; planning decisions 51; property taxes 50; public housing 44, 54, 57; reformers 70; regulations 51; *in rem* buildings 58–59; rental types 54; rental vs. ownership 53, 54, 55, 57; rent-stabilized housing 54, 57; settlement houses 69; supply/demand 47, 49–58, 81, 90; Tenant Interim Lease Program (TIL) 59; Tenement House Committees 70; vacancy rates 56–58, 90; Work(ing)men's Home (1855) 69; *see also* housing units: *individual boroughs*
Housing Act (1937) 81
housing activism 58–59, 69–70
housing cost burden 55, 57, 100
Housing Development Fund Companies (HDFCs) 59
Housing New York 2.0 (2017) (Mayor B. de Blasio) 59, 60–61
Housing New York: A Five-Borough Ten-year Housing Plan (2014) (Mayor B. de Blasio) 60

housing plans (mayoral) 59–60, 100
housing unit density 48
housing units 48–49, 57; *City of Yes for Housing Opportunity* (COYFHA) 100–101; Co-op City (Bronx) 70, 95; rehabilitation/construction of 59–61, 91, 94; single room occupancy (SRO) buildings 82; subdivision of 82; substandard 82
Houston Street (south of) 13
Howe, Elias 19
Hudson River 8, 13, 18, 49, 84, 89
Hudson Square 21
hydroelectric dams 80

image (of NYC) 72–77
immigrant neighborhoods 30, 31–32; Bronx 94–95; Harlem 93–94; Lower East Side 89–91; Queens 96–97
immigrants: business ownership 31; conflict with residents 29; education level 31, 90; support for 29, 69–70; undocumented 27, 28–29
immigration: arrival and settlement 27–29, 31–32; employment 29–30, 89–90; and housing demand 53; numbers 26–28, 30–31; points of entry 27, 29; reasons for 26–28, 30, 90; waves 53
Immigration Act (1924) 27, 90
Immigration Act (1990) 27
Immigration and Nationality (Hart–Cellar) Act (1965) 27, 30
Immigration and Reform Control Act (IRCA) (1986) 27
income: household 53, 55; renter 54
Independent Budget Office (IBO) 42, 62
Indian immigrants 97

Industrial Business Zones (IBZs) 23
industry: film and television industry 22; garment/fashion industry 16–17, 18–20, 29, 71, 90; location quotients (LQ) 33–34; machinery industry 17; manufacturing 16–17, 18, 23–24, 29, 37, 84, 87; media industry 22, 24; printing and publishing 21–22; publishing industry 24, 77; sugar production 18; *see also* employment
infrastructure (decaying) 38
infrastructure projects 80–82
in rem buildings 58–59
institutional facilities 78
intellectuals 92
Interborough Rapid Transit (IRT) Company 68
International Ladies Garment Workers Union (ILGWU) 71
international reputation *see* reputation (international)
interstate system 17
Irish immigrants 29–30, 32, 89
Irving, Washington: *Salmagundi* 4
Italian immigrants 30, 32, 89

Jackson, Reggie 45
Jamaican immigrants 31
James Corner Field Operations 52
Jazzmobile, Harlem 92
jazz musicians 92, 96
Jewish Communal Fund 35
Jewish National Workers Alliance 71
Jewish population 26, 88, 95
John F. Kennedy airport 66
Jones Beach State Park 80
JPMorgan Chase Foundation 35

Kessner, Thomas 2
Kingsbridge Heights (Bronx) 48

Kleindeutschland 89
knowledge-based economy 17, 24, 84
Koch, Mayor Ed 59; *Ten-year Housing Plan* (1985) 59–60, 95
Korean immigrants 29, 30, 31
Kulkarni, Rajendra: map of Metropolitan Statistical Area (MSA) 6; overview of New York City's boroughs 7

labor laws 79
labor organizations 71
LaGuardia airport 35, 66
LaGuardia, Mayor Fiorello 1, 70, 79, 81
land market 13
land use 51, 77, 84
Latin American immigrants 30–31
Le Corbusier 77
LeFrak family 34, 71
legislative process (local government) 63
Lehman, Governor Herbert H. 79
Lenapehoking 10
Leni Lenape 10
Lenox Avenue/Malcolm X Boulevard 14, 15
Lexington Avenue 14, 15
libraries (public) 42–43, 51
Life magazine 21
light (natural) 15
Lincoln Center for the Performing Arts 78, 80
Lincoln Theater, Harlem 92
Lincoln Tunnel 66–67
Lindsay, Mayor John 4; Mayor's Office of Film, Theater, and Broadcasting (MOFTB) 22
Little Italy 89, 92
Little Odessa 89
Liverpool 8

local development organizations 71–72
Local Law 45 (1976) 58
location (New York City): advantages of 2, 5, 8–9; disadvantages of 9; economic development 84; and housing supply 49–50; Hudson River estuary 8; Metropolitan Statistical Area (MSA) 5, 6; trade routes 5
location quotients (LQ) 33–34
London 12, 33, 86
Long Island 79
Long Island Sound 5
Long Island State Park Commission 79
Look magazine 21
Lord & Taylor [department store] 20
Los Angeles 26
lots (dimensions of) 16
low-end jobs 37
Lower East Side 24, 50, 71, 94; "Alphabet City" 91; Cooper Square Committee 83; crime 91; ethic clusters 89–91; fire services 43; gentrification 91; housing 90–91; Neighborhood Guild 69; population density 48
lower-income residents 16, 38–39, 43, 60–61
Lower Manhattan *see* Manhattan
low-income ("gig") economy 17

McCarthy, Senator Joseph 71
machinery industry 17
Macy's 20
"Made in NY" Discount Card 23
"Made in NY" Marketing Credit program 23
Madison Avenue 14, 15, 24
Madison Avenue Bridge 87

magazines 21
Manhattan 11–12, 92; Alliance for Downtown New York 72, 76; bridges 66, 68; Central Business District 64; congestion pricing 64; cultural attractions 52; downtown 49–50, 77, 91–92; finance and economy 91; Financial District 24, 92; horizontal vs. vertical expansion 13; housing 88, 89; (immigrant) population 12, 32, 48, 88–89; impact of austerity measures 43; Lower Manhattan 91; parks 52; skyscrapers 49; transport links 68; *see also* Lower East Side: Midtown
Manhattan Bridge 68
Manhattan Heliport 66
Manhattan schist (bedrock) 49
Manhattantown redevelopment 83–84
manufacturing: blue-collar 16–17, 84; Brooklyn 87; decrease in 17; employment 17, 23, 29, 37, 38; locations 23–24; sugar production 18; *see also* garment industry
maps: Metropolitan Statistical Area (MSA) *6*; New York City's boroughs *7*
marine terminals *see* port terminals
marketing campaigns 72, 74–77
AMay Laws 90
mayoral housing plans 59–60
mayor (role of) 62
Mayor's Committee on Slum Clearance *see* Slum Clearance Committee (SCC)
Mayor's Office of Film, Theater, and Broadcasting (MOFTB) 22
Mayor's Office of Media and Entertainment (MOME) 22

media industry 22, 24
metropolitan divisions 5
Metropolitan Museum of Art ("Met") 35
Metropolitan Statistical Area (MSA) 5, *6*, 64
Metropolitan Transportation Authority (MTA) 38, 42, 68, 84
Mexican immigrants 31
middle-income residents 43, 44, 50; housing 16, 60–61, 81, 91; migrants 30
Midtown 24; manufacturing 24; office district 22, 49, 92; parks 52; printing and publishing industry 21–22; skyscrapers 49–50
migration 53
Minuit, Peter 11
Mitchell, Mayor John Purroy 78
Molotch, H. 71
Montgomerie Charter 12
Montgomerie, Governor John 12
Morgan, J. P. 35
Morris, Gouverneur [Founding Father] 12
Moses, Robert 77–84; career 78–80, 83–84; defeats 83; displacement (of residents) 82, 83, 84; infrastructure projects 80–81; reputation and investigation into 83–84; state parks 80–81
Moshulu (Bronx) 48
movies *see* film industry
Mumford, Lewis 70
Municipal Assistance Corporation (MAC) 40–41
municipal bonds 39, 40–42
municipal function expenditures 40
municipal housing 39
Municipal Water Finance Authority 60

murals 35
Museum of Modern Art (MoMA) 35, 52
museums 35, 52; National Jazz Museum, Harlem 92
musicians 36
mutual aid societies 29

names (of streets/avenues) 13–14
National Broadcasting Company (NBC) *see* NBC (National Broadcasting Company)
National Housing Act (1934) 58
National Housing Conference (NHC) 70
National Jazz Museum, Harlem 92
native tribes 10
natural light 15
NBC (National Broadcasting Company) 23
neighborhood attachment 3
Neighborhood Guild (Lower East Side) 69
neighborhoods *see* immigrant neighborhoods
New Amsterdam 11
Newark Liberty International airport 66
Newark, New Jersey (port terminal) 66, 67
New Deal 43
New Housing Marketplace Plan (NHMP) (2003) (Mayor M. Bloomberg) 59, 60
New Jersey 64, 66
New Netherland 11
Newspaper Row (Printing House Square) 21
newspapers 21
New York Academy of Art 45
New York Chamber of Commerce 74

New York City: Charter Revision 51; in city rankings 33–34; in competition with Philadelphia 2–3; as de facto/de jure/state capital 16; finance and economy 91; location/infrastructure 2–3, 8; nicknames 4, 34, 35; praise for 1–3; *see also* New Amsterdam: population
New York City Charter 86
New York City Council 62, 63
New York City Economic Development Corporation (NYCEDC) 71, 72
New York City Housing and Vacancy Survey (NYCHVS) 56–57
New York City Housing Authority (NYCHA) 80, 82–83
New York City Housing Development Corporation (NYCHDC) 60
New York City Industrial Development Agency (NYCIDA) 73–74
New York City Marketing (NYCM) 72
New York City Partnership (NYCP) *see* Partnership for New York City
New York City Police Department (NYPD) 42, 43, 45–46
New York City Tunnel Authority 79
New York Community Trust 35
The New Yorker magazine 21
New York Herald Tribune 21
New York Park Association: Metropolitan Conference on Parks 79
New York Post 45
New York Public Library 16
New York School (of art) 35

New York State: Commissioners' Plan (1811) 12–13, 14–16; Council of Parks 79; Department of Commerce 75; Financial Control Board (NYSFCB) 41–42; Financial Emergency Act (FEA) 40; government 63–64; housing unit density 48; Legislature 35; population density 48; Post Production Tax Credit Program 22; property taxes 50
New York State Insurance Code (1938) 81
New York Stock Exchange (NYSE) 34, 36
New York Times 21
New York Yankees 45, 95
nicknames 4, 34, 35
non-Hispanic White population 26, 78; conflict with Chinese immigrants 29; Harlem 93, 94; housing 56; Queens 96
north-south avenues 13–14
numbers (of streets) 13
NYC & Company 72, 76
NYC Big Events 72

Occupy Wall Street (OWS) 99
O'Dwyer, Mayor 79
oil price crisis (1973/4) 37
Olmsted, Frederick Law 15, 52
open spaces 79; *see also* parks
Operation Lone Star 28
Order Sons of Italy in America 29
Organization of Petroleum Exporting Countries (OPEC) 37
Orthodox Jews 88
Oudolf, Piet 52
outer boroughs 86
Outerbridge Crossing 66
Outerbridge, Eugenius Harvey 66

"packet ships" 8
Paris, France 12, 25, 86
Park Avenue 14, 15
Parker, Dorothy: "My Home Town" 1
parking requirements 100
parks 15, 52; Bronx 94; Central Park 15, 24, 52, 76; funding for 51; High Line, Manhattan 52; Metropolitan Conference on Parks (New York Park Association) 79; state parks 80
parkways 80
Parson's School of Design 20
Partnership for New York City 72, 74
peddling carts *see* street vendors
Pennsylvania Station 16, 21, 46, 92
per capita common function debt 39–40
Philadelphia 2–3, 8; population 12, 25, 87; port facilities 5, 8
philanthropists 35, 69–70
photographers 92, 94
piano factories (Bronx) 94
Pink, Louis 70
Plan (1811) *see under* New York State
PlaNYC 2030: A Greener, Greater New York 99
plazas 13
poets 92
Poet's Den Theater, Harlem 92
police officers *see* New York City Police Department (NYPD)
Polish immigrants 30
population 25–28, 30–31, 47, 100; after consolidation of boroughs 86; loss 26, 38; NYC vs. other cities 12, 25; *see also* boroughs
population density 47–48
Port Authority of New York and New Jersey (PANYNJ) 60, 64, 66–67

Port Authority Trans-Hudson (PATH) railroad 67
port facilities 66; immigrant workforce 29, 89; NYC vs. Philadelphia 5, 8; transportation of goods 8–9
Port of New York Authority *see* Port Authority of New York and New Jersey (PANYNJ)
port terminals 66, 67
Post Office Complex 21
poverty (household) 56, 93; *see also* lower-income residents
praise (for New York) 1–3
Pratt Institute 20, 80
printing industry 21–22, 30
professional services sector 17
property taxes: abatements 50, 73–74; delinquency 58; exemptions 34; New York State 50
Prospect Park, Brooklyn 52
Provisional Orders (WIC) 11
Public Advocate 62, 63
Public Development Corporation *see* New York City Economic Development Corporation (NYCEDC)
public housing 44, 54, 57, 90
Public Housing Conference (1931) 70
public–private partnerships (PPPs) 72
public sector employment 38
public services (fiscal crises) 37, 39–40
public spaces 15
public squares 13, 15
Public Works Administration (PWA) 81
publishing industry 21–22, 24, 77
Puerto Ricans 90–91, 94

quality-of-life campaign 45–46
Queens 95; conflict between immigrants and residents 29; ethnic/racial diversity 96–97; Flushing 29; gridiron (street grid) 13; housing 96; (immigrant) population 32, 95, 96–97; postal address 95–96; small batch (garment) production 20; street layout 96; transport links 68; urbanization and gentrification 97; World's Fair, Flushing Meadows 77, 79, 80
Queensboro Bridge 68, 95

racial diversity 26; *see also individual boroughs*
racial segregation 82, 93, 96
Radio City Music Hall 23
radio stations 23
railroads 66, 67
rankings (of cities) 33
ready-to-wear (prêt-à-porter) clothes 19
real estate 34, 71; arson 26, 43, 44, 58; blockbusting 88; business improvement districts (BID) 73; economic challenges 38; New York City Economic Development Corporation (NYCEDC) 71, 72; Regional Plan Association (RPA) 65; rehabilitation (of housing) 59–61, 91, 94; subsidies 72; *see also* housing
rebranding (of NYC) 72–75
recessions *see* economy
Reconstruction Finance Corporation 79
recreation activities (development of) 79
redevelopment 83; *see also* development organizations

Redevelopment Companies Law (RCL) 81
redlining 88
Regional Plan Association (RPA) 65, 86
Regional Plan of New York and Its Environs (1929) 65, 86
regional plans 65, 86; *see also* Regional Plan Association (RPA)
rehabilitation (of housing) 59–61, 91, 94
Related Group 71
religious diversity 26
rent burden 55, 56
rentership rate 54
rent-stabilized housing 54, 57
reputation (international) 2
resilience 100
Riis, Jacob 94
Rockefeller Center 24
Rockefeller, David 74, 76
Rockefeller Foundation 65
Rockefeller, Governor Nelson 84
Roebling, John Augustus 68
Roosevelt Island 68
Rose family 71
Rudin family 71
Russian immigrants/population 30, 88, 89
Ruthurford, John 12

Safe Streets/Safe City program 45
Sanders, James 3–4
sanitation 42, 43
San Juan Hill neighborhood (displacement from) 78
Savoy Ballroom, Harlem 92
Schomburg Center for Research in Black Culture 93
Scottish immigrants 30
Second Regional Plan (1968) 65
Secretary of State (for New York) 79

segregation (racial) 82, 93, 96
Senate Committee on Banking and Commerce 83
Seneca Village 15
September 11 attacks 3–4, 76
service sector employment 17, 23, 37
settlement houses 69
settlers 11
Seventh Avenue (Adam Clayton Powell Jr. Boulevard) 14, 15, 24
Shea Stadium 80
shipbuilding 8
shipping (container shipping) 66, 67
shipping services (scheduled) 8
shopping (high-end) 24
sidewalks 15
signature events 76
Simkhovitch, Mary Kingsbury 70
Singer, Isaac 19
single room occupancy (SRO) buildings 82
Sixth Avenue (Lenox Avenue, Malcolm X Boulevard) 14
skyscrapers (location of) 49–50
slaves 11–12
Sloan, John 3
Slum Clearance Committee (SCC) 79–80, 82
Smalls Paradise Club, Harlem 92
Smith, Governor Alfred E. 79
socioeconomic inequality (impact of) 99–100
SoHa (South of Harlem) 94
SoHo 49, 92
Solomon R. Guggenheim Museum 35
Son of Sam murders 44
South Bronx *see* Bronx (Bronx County)
Soviet Union 30
"Spanish Harlem" *see* Harlem

squares (public) 13, 15
Starrett family 71
State Emergency Public Works Commission 79
state government 63
Staten Island (Richmond County) 97; bridges 66, 67–68; housing 97; immigrant population 32; port facilities 66; transport links 97
state parks 80
Stein, Clarence 70
stock market crash (1987) 36
stop and frisk 46
storms (coastal) 99
street grid (gridiron) 13, 96
street layout 13, 15, 96
street names 13–14
street vendors 30, 31
strikes 43
Stuyvesant, Peter 11
Stuyvesant Town/Turtle Bay 48, 92
subsidies 72
suburbs (move to) 58, 82
subway 68, 93
sugar production 16, 18
sunlight 15
superblocks 13, 15
Superstorm Sandy 3

taxes 12; austerity measures 42–43; property taxes 34, 50, 58, 73–74; tax cuts/incentives 43, 73–74
teachers 42
television industry 22, 75–76, 77
television stations 23
Tenant Interim Lease Program (TIL) 59
Tenement House Act (1901) ("New Law") 70
Tenement House Committees 70
tenement laws 70
tenements 89
Tenth Avenue (Amsterdam Avenue) 14
Tenth Street School of Abstract Expressionists *see* New York School (of art)
Ten-year Housing Plan (1985) (Mayor Ed Koch) 59–60, 95
Teterboro, New Jersey 66
Texas: Operation Lone Star 28
Third Avenue Bridge 87
Third Regional Plan (1996) 65
Thomas, Norman 70
Time magazine 21
Times Square 21, 24, 73
Times Square District 91–92
Tishman family 34
Tishman-Speyer family 71
Title I funding 81–82, 84
toll booths/revenues 81
Tompkins Square Park, Manhattan 52
topographical features 14
tourism 76, 77; *see also* visitor numbers
tourist attractions 35
trade 11–12; *see also* goods
trade routes 5
traffic congestion 50, 64
transportation: airports 66; bridges 66–68, 80; elevated transit line 68; expressways 80–81; mass transportation 50, 66; Metropolitan Transport Authority (MTA) 38, 42; railroads 67; subway 68, 93
Tribeca (TRIangle BElow CAnal) 45, 92
Triborough Bridge and Tunnel Authority (TBTA) 79, 81, 84
Triborough Bridge Authority (TBA) 79, 81

Trinidad and Tobago (immigrants from) 31
Trump family 71
Trump, Fred 34
tunnels 66–67, 95

Uniform Land Use Review Process (ULURP) 51
unions 71; economic impact of 37, 38; garment industry 71; high unionization rate 50, 71
United Housing Foundation (UHF) 70
United Nations Headquarters 16, 78, 80
United Workers' Association (UWA) 71
universities (campus expansion) 78, 80
University Heights Bridge 87
University Settlement Society of New York 69
Upper East Side 24, 48, 89
upper-income residents 9, 50, 81, 91
Upper Manhattan *see* Manhattan
Upper West Side 14
Uptown *see* Harlem
urban decay 94
Urban Homesteading Assistance Board (UHAB) 58
urbanization 87, 97
urban land parcels 71
urban planning: financing 81–82; Regional Plan of New York and Its Environs (1929) 65; Robert Moses 77–84; *see also under* New York State
urban renewal programs 78, 93
Urquhart, Brian [UN Under-Secretary-General] 2

vacancy rates (housing) 56–58, 90
Vanderbilt, Cornelius 35

Vaux, Calvert 15, 52
Veiller, Lawrence 70
Vergara, Camilo José: *Harlem: The Unmaking of a Ghetto* 94
vertical expansion (Manhattan) 13
visitor numbers 38, 76
Vonnegut, Kurt 88
Vornado Realty Trust 71

Wagner, Mayor Robert F. 79, 83
Wald, Lilian 70
Wallace, Mike 2
Wall Street 11–12, 24, 34, 92
warehouses 29, 87, 89
Warhol, Andy 45
"Warhol economy" 36
Washington Square 21
Washington Square Park 50
waste collection 15
wealth: high-net-worth individuals 34, 53; household 53
weather 5, 8, 99
welfare benefits 38–39, 42
Welfare Island *see* Roosevelt Island
Welsh immigrants 30
West African immigrants 93–94
West Indies (trade with) 11–12
West Side 92
West Side Urban Renewal Area 84
West Village 92
white-collar employment 17
White, E. B. 4; *Here is New York* 1
White flight (to suburbs) 58
White-owned establishments 93
Whitney Museum 35
width (of avenues) 15
Williamsburg Bridge 68
Williamsburg, Brooklyn 18, 24, 87
Willis Avenue Bridge 87
Wise, Rabbi Steven 70
Wood, Edith Elmer 70
Work(ing)men's Home (1855) 69

Works Progress Administration (WPA) 35, 81
World's Fair, Flushing Meadows, Queens (1939/1940 & 1964/1965) 77, 79, 80
World Trade Center 66–67, 75, 76
World War I (and immigration) 27
World War II (and immigration) 27, 53
writers 92

Yankees *see* New York Yankees
Yiddishist Cooperative Heimgesellschaft 71
Yom Kippur War 37
Yorkville, Manhattan 89

Zeckendorf family 71
zero tolerance 46
zoning 86, 100–101

For Product Safety Concerns and Information please contact our EU representative GPSR@taylorandfrancis.com
Taylor & Francis Verlag GmbH, Kaufingerstraße 24, 80331 München, Germany

www.ingramcontent.com/pod-product-compliance
Lightning Source LLC
Chambersburg PA
CBHW070938180426
43192CB00039B/2323